A HOUGHTON LIBRARY

CHRONICLE

1942–1992

A HOUGHTON LIBRARY
CHRONICLE
1942–1992

HARVARD COLLEGE LIBRARY

CAMBRIDGE · MASSACHUSETTS

1992

Cover: Architects' design for a capital in the Houghton Exhibition Room.
Title page: Design for plaque in Lobby.

Courtesy of Perry Dean Rogers & Partners, Boston, Massachusetts
(formerly Perry, Shaw and Hepburn)

TO THE COLLEAGUES, FRIENDS, AND

READERS THAT HOUGHTON HAS

BROUGHT TOGETHER

1942–1992

PREFACE

Capturing the history of a busy institution such as the Houghton Library poses substantial challenges to those who attempt it. The Library's well-known annual reports, first written by William Jackson when Houghton opened, focused on acquisitions, and even these reports were discontinued fifteen years ago; comprehensive narrative reports on *all* aspects of the Library's activities and mission were introduced only two years ago. The Library's publishing record, changes in personnel, and the accumulation of endowed funds can be traced with some confidence (if not always with some ease), but the sheer number of lectures and exhibitions is daunting, particularly given the Library's increasing role as a center for teaching. It is therefore with some trepidation—but not without a great deal of pleasure—that we offer our friends a tentative chronicle of the first fifty years of the rare book and manuscript library of Harvard College.

This chronicle has been compiled by three senior members of the Library's staff: Hugh Amory, Senior Cataloguer; Elizabeth Falsey, Associate Curator of Manuscripts; and Nancy Finlay, Associate Curator of Printing and Graphic Arts. They have worked for the most part from printed sources, such as the *Harvard Library Bulletin* and the *Harvard University Library Notes;* these have been supplemented by the records of the Library Personnel Office (unfortunately not complete for this period), by library telephone directories, by interviews, and by copious collections of photographs. The *Chronicle* is largely a record of people, not of books, and it can only suggest the transformation of a Treasure Room, containing about 100,000 volumes, into a center for research, involving 500,000. And as Hugh, Betty and Nancy would be the first to attest, this is indeed a communal effort: corrections and additions are welcome, although the next edition probably awaits our 75th anniversary.

Among those who shared their memories with the Chroniclers, special thanks are due to William Bentinck-Smith, Rodney G. Dennis, Lawrence Dowler, Eleanor M. Garvey, Rae Ann Nager, Frederica H. Oldach, James E. Walsh, and Edwin E. Williams. Catherine Johnson and Jeanne T. Newlin provided perspective on the Harvard Theatre Collection. Wallace F. Dailey, Katharine F. Pantzer, and Michael Winship helped to document the Theodore Roosevelt Collection, the *STC* and the *BAL*, respectively. Dennis Marnon and Roger Stoddard both assisted with compiling lists of endowed funds as well as in many other ways. Further invaluable assistance came from Harley P. Holden and Robin McElheny in the Harvard University Archives and from Joan Nordell, the Assistant Director for External Affairs in the University Library. Two of our colleagues deserve particular recognition. Carolyn Jakeman long served as the legendary keeper of the Houghton Reading Room, where she kept a watchful (and helpful) eye on generations of scholars young and old. What her readers never imagined was that, as a prolific photographer, she quickly emerged as the unofficial keeper of the flame, chronicling the Library's personal and professional fortunes for thirty-four years. To her we owe renewed gratitude for her eagerness in sharing her memories (and photographs) with us. And to William H. Bond, the second Librarian of the

Houghton Library, we owe an immense debt for his continuing effort to capture the early history of an institution and the scholars who shaped it. Wonderfully clear and precise essays and appreciations have already appeared on Arthur Houghton, William Jackson, and Philip Hofer. We are delighted that another informative piece by Bill Bond introduces this volume.

RICHARD WENDORF, *Librarian*

CONTENTS

THE HOUGHTON LIBRARY

NOTES ON ITS ORIGIN AND DEVELOPMENT

The Library that Never Was: Preliminary View.
Courtesy Perry Dean Rogers & Partners, Boston, Massachusetts
(formerly Perry, Shaw and Hepburn)

Arthur Amory Houghton, Jr.
Photograph by Dorothy Wilding

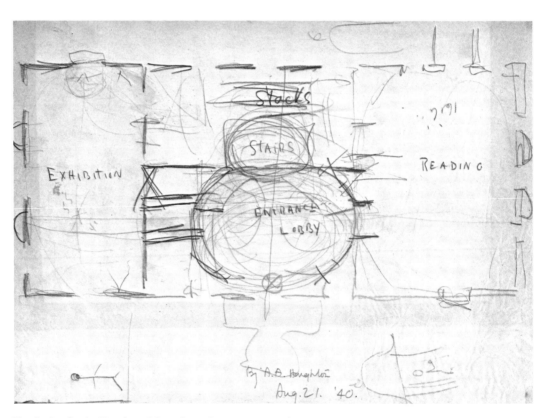

Sketch plan for the Houghton Library by Arthur Amory Houghton, Jr.

THE HOUGHTON LIBRARY

NOTES ON ITS ORIGIN AND DEVELOPMENT

In September 1937, when Keyes DeWitt Metcalf began eighteen years of distinguished service as Director of the Harvard University Library and Librarian of Harvard College, he correctly perceived that his first task was to acquaint himself as rapidly as possible with the staff, the collections, and the physical plant of the library. He found that the collections of the College Library were extraordinarily strong but that the Harry Elkins Widener Memorial Library, which housed them, was full to bursting (as indeed it still is, despite many shifts and changes, considerable decentralization and remote storage, and the creation of new facilities within the College Yard). Continued growth is a fact of life in all great research libraries. Various expedients can reduce its rate but not eliminate it.

Collections also require protection. Widener Library was completed and dedicated in 1915, long before the days of air conditioning; already the humidity of summer, the dry heat of winter, and the ever more pervasive pollution from the city environment were placing its nearly two million volumes at hazard. Microforms and computerization, which were to come later as the great innovations of the past fifty years, do not (as many fondly hoped) solve the problems of space and preservation. They provide great convenience and efficiency for certain library uses as well as essential ancillary functions but, in fact, they increase the many responsibilities of the research library and make additional demands on its resources of personnel, space, and funds, while for many scholarly purposes they cannot substitute for the book or manuscript itself.

By March 1938, Metcalf placed before the Harvard Corporation three proposals designed to mitigate the problems he perceived: a separate building with climate control to house rare books and manuscripts, connected to Widener by a tunnel and a bridge; another adjacent library designed specifically for undergraduate use; and a cooperative storage facility for less-used books, to be shared with other libraries in the Boston area. These proposals were speedily endorsed by the Corporation, but with the usual Harvard *caveat:* the funds to carry them out must be raised by the proposer. No obvious prospects for financing were immediately perceptible. It is to Metcalf's enduring credit that within ten years the Houghton and Lamont Libraries were built with the gifts of generous donors, and the New England Deposit Library was constructed under a mortgage that was paid off five years earlier than expected through rent collected from institutions using the building.

Mr. Metcalf writes of these matters and much more in his autobiographical *My Harvard Library Years* (Cambridge, 1988), and it is clear that the planning and financing of much-needed buildings did not divert him from the effort to recruit and support the strongest staff he could assemble. Several senior positions needed to be filled, more were scheduled to fall vacant through retirement, and the evolving needs for library services required the creation of new posts. His first important appointment was that of William Alexander Jackson as Associate Professor of Bibliography and Assistant Librarian in charge of the rare book collection. Jackson had caught the virus of books and bibliography when a boy in California, the next door neighbor of Dr. George Watson Cole, first librarian of the Huntington Library. As an undergraduate at Williams College he worked on an elaborate and highly professional catalogue of the rare books in the Chapin Collection in the college library; but for the coming of the Great Depression, it would have been published. He was then commissioned to compile an even more elaborate catalogue of the private collection of Carl H. Pforzheimer, Sr., which he had carried to completion and seen through page proof. He knew librarians, collectors, and booksellers on both sides of the Atlantic, and had begun the mammoth task of revising Pollard and Redgrave's *Short-Title Catalogue* (London, 1929) of books printed in England or in English to the year 1640. At the age of thirty-three he was already recognized as a world-class bibliographer.

The appointment was made despite vigorous opposition from the then Chairman of the Library's Visiting Committee, the constitutional lawyer Charles Warren, who felt that the University had no business acquiring and caring for rare books and manuscripts, and that a librarian to look after such things was certainly not needed. Metcalf did not agree, and his arguments carried the day. Jackson joined the staff on September 1, 1938. With him came his close friend Philip Hofer, '21, a young and enthusiastic connoisseur and collector, previously on the staffs of the New York Public and Pierpont Morgan Libraries. It proved to be a momentous day for the Harvard Library.

Jackson set to work at once learning the contents of the Treasure Room collection (as it was then called) and plucking from the general stacks unrecognized books that were at risk because of their rarity and value, a function much desired by Metcalf, who was aware that the general collections had already suffered too much from the depredations of both casual and professional thieves. Jackson also reinforced Metcalf's view that the environment of Widener stacks—from which rare books and manuscripts were separated only by a wire mesh cage—was unsuitable for the conservation of such materials.

Another task was to promote their use in the University curriculum; they were not to be curiosities for display only. Bibliography and book collecting had been subjects of study at Harvard for a good many years. On his own and in partnership with Hofer, Jackson brought a new degree of professionalism and enthusiasm to the courses he taught in addition to his other duties. Thus began a tradition of teaching that today is shared by many more members of the staff. Hofer also began the facsimile publication of some of the unique treasures of the Library, another practice that still continues.

Meantime Hofer, who had brought with him his already considerable private collection, established the Department of Printing and Graphic Arts, the first such in any major library, and served for many years as its first Curator at a nominal salary. (Not until Paul Buck, wise in the ways of administration, became Director of the University Library was the Curator's salary raised to a realistic level. Buck clearly foresaw the budgetary shock that would suddenly occur when Hofer retired and a replacement would have to be found. Today the position is wholly supported by a fund raised in memory of Philip Hofer by his many friends, colleagues, and students.)

Another momentous appointment, made in 1938 at Jackson's suggestion, was that of Arthur Amory Houghton, Jr., '29 to the Library Visiting Committee. Houghton was already a major collector, especially of books and manuscripts by John Keats and of English literature of the sixteenth to eighteenth centuries. At the first committee meeting that Houghton attended, Metcalf once more stated the case for a climate-controlled building to house rare books and manuscripts, and Charles Warren predictably attacked the collection of such materials by the University. Jackson, who had prepared for such an eventuality, rose with an eloquent defense. Among other things, he pointed out that no rare books or manuscripts were acquired with the unrestricted income of the University, and that these resources were irreplaceable and genuinely at risk. Somewhat mollified, Warren did not continue his attack, but he had obviously upset Arthur Houghton. To Warren's credit, it should be said that ten years later he left a munificent bequest to the University, a considerable portion of which was designated to support the Library's collections in American history—but not of rare materials.

After the meeting Houghton asked Jackson and Hofer to join him in his hotel room, where they discussed the situation far into the night. They agreed that the three of them should set out on a protracted but highly selective fund-raising tour to insure the financing of the new building at the earliest moment; but by next morning when Houghton returned to Cambridge to confer with Metcalf, Jackson, and Hofer, he had made up his mind to give a block of Corning Glass stock, previously a family-held company, sufficient to plan and build the library that now bears his name. And the planning began at once; in the shadow of the European war there was no time to be lost.

Arthur Houghton (himself an architect *manqué*) recommended as architect William G. Perry of the Boston firm of Perry, Shaw and Hepburn, who had designed Houghton's own private library in Maryland. Perry had a national reputation through his reconstruction of Colonial Williamsburg, and the Corporation approved his selection. The new library was to be built into the slope of the hill east of Widener, was to be insulated and double-glazed throughout and made of the finest materials and with the best workmanship available. The engineering pressed forward with such speed that the most important structural members were safely in hand before wartime priorities began to limit construction in the United States; nevertheless some compromises proved necessary. Thus the elegant balconies outside the windows of the main floor, apparently of wrought iron, were actually made of wood, and the forbidding bars protecting the ground floor windows were also wooden (they, however, have been replaced by steel). The air conditioning was state-of-the-art, the air being cooled, washed, and passed through charcoal filters and an electronic device, to be delivered at a constant temperature and humidity. Over the course of fifty years, of course, machinery was worn out or obsolesced, and there have been radical changes in the techniques of heating, ventilation, and air conditioning; the Houghton Library begins its second half-century with a thoroughly renovated system meeting the highest current standards.

Accommodation for the books and manuscripts received no less careful attention. The exhibition cases and many of the glass-fronted shelves in public areas were lit with cold-cathode tubes to prevent overheating, and wherever possible were tied in with the air conditioning system. The metal shelving in the stacks was designed with no sharp corners or edges to injure the books, and received four coats of baked enamel, each rubbed and polished before the next was applied. Alas, such meticulous work is no longer economically feasible, and each subsequent extension of the stack area shows a gradual decline in its shelving, though it is the best that could be afforded at the time of installation.

A visitor entering the building today sees much the same vista as he or she would have in 1942 when the library was dedicated. A few of the "permanent" displays in the wall cases of the oval lobby have been replaced, and the large chandeliers that used to overheat the Reading Room have been replaced by cooler fluorescent lights. Behind the scenes, glass-fronted cases originally held the library's entire collection of *Short-Title Catalogue* books, but they have long since moved to the sub-basement area of the stack; the cases house bibliographical reference books supplementing those in the Reading Room, and the area contains desks where the Reading Room staff deals with the ever-increasing load of reference questions and photo orders. A mezzanine behind the Reading Room clock still houses the cataloguers of printed books and their shelf-lists.

Only the north end of the upper floor of the library was fully finished when it opened; the Keats Room and its curator's office, the Amy Lowell Collection (transferred from the top floor of Widener), and a large seminar room that has served many functions: housing the Emerson Papers while they were being sorted and indexed, providing an office for Jacob Blanck and his assistants and successors to work on the *Bibliography of American Literature*, and office and work space for various other purposes. At the southwest corner was the room commissioned and paid for by William King Richardson, 1880, to hold his remarkable collection of early manuscripts, incunabula, and fine bindings; though finished, it remained vacant and was used as temporary working space until Mr. Richardson's death in 1951 brought the bequest of his books to fill its shelves. A long corridor with locked glass cases connected the Richardson Room with the north end of the building, and it housed such collections as Harris Kennedy's collection of Lafcadio Hearn and the Livingston collection of Kipling—books, be it admitted, that were somewhat hastily selected to fill the shelves in time for the opening of the library. When the Emily Dickinson Collection came with the requirement that a special room be provided for books and furniture from the Dickinson home, a floor was installed in an unused elevator shaft off the corridor for the purpose. The area to the east and south of the corridor was completely unfinished, with the intention that it could eventually be remodeled to house some important collection or collections. Today, the corridor has disappeared, with the construction of the Hyde Rooms with their offices and seminar room; the Emily Dickinson Room is in the space formerly occupied by the Lowell Collection, which has moved to more commodious quarters on the west side next to the Richardson Room.

On the office floor, immediately below the main entrance, the Librarian's office is still at the north end of the corridor and the Curator of Printing and Graphic Arts holds sway at the south end; but there has been much rearrangement and reassignment of the intervening spaces, to accommodate increased staff and changing functions, and the inevitable electronic equipment. The original "back stack," an area used for unpacking and sorting new acquisitions and storing them for accessioning, has undergone several remodelings; first into an elaborately decorated suite of three rooms and a foyer for Theatre Collection displays when that department moved from Widener to Houghton; and when it in turn moved to new quarters in the Pusey Library, the rooms were torn out and replaced by offices and work space for the Manuscript Department. The rationale for these arrangements still continues: to promote easy and informal consultation among staff members, and to place them in close proximity to the collections for which they are responsible.

The two floors below the office level contain locked stacks and a vault. They communicate through a tunnel with the lowest level of Widener and through doors to two underground levels of the Pusey Library. Such communication was anticipated when Houghton was planned, with a special panel in the southeast corner of the foundation designed to be easily removed when needed. When Lamont Library opened in 1955, the upper of its two levels of underground stacks was designated for the expansion of Houghton, and a long sloping tunnel led, as planned, from one building to the other. The building of Pusey forced the destruction of this tunnel, and internal communication with the Lamont stacks is now through the portion of Pusey stacks assigned to Houghton use.

The original Houghton building was essentially complete in the autumn of 1941, and the transfer of materials from the old Treasure Room and its stacks was begun. As has frequently been the case, it was a do-it-yourself operation. The Treasure Room staff, never overlarge, loaded book-trucks and wheeled them on and off the elevators and across the bridge to deposit their contents in their new home. Jackson and Hofer and their secretaries pitched in personally, joined by Carolyn Jakeman, supervisor of the Reading Room, and W. H. McCarthy, Jr., Jackson's first assistant, plus whatever personnel could be conscripted for the service. In the nature of things, much of this work was done at night or during weekends so as not to interfere with normal library functions. After a substantial portion of the collection had been moved, and before the official opening of the library, scholars began using the new Reading Room.

The same small staff had to plan suitable dedicatory ceremonies and fitting exhibitions and publications, work out guest lists, and circulate invitations. Jackson wrote and published an illustrated pamphlet describing the building and its contents; Thomas Matthews, the legendary first doorman of the Houghton Library, addressed the invitations by hand.

This "home industry" aspect of the move into the new library and the preparations for its dedication, necessitated by budgetary limitations on the size of its staff, placed considerable burdens on those involved. At the same time it created a sense of involvement and the *esprit de corps* that have pervaded the Houghton Library during most of its history. Hardly any of the many persons who have served there, regardless of level, have failed to lend a hand whenever and wherever needed. Librarians, cataloguers, Reading Room attendants, all have turned to when a job needed to be done, from wrapping and packing books in a private library for shipment to Houghton, driving a rented truck transporting them, hand-addressing annual appeals to Friends of the Library, to mopping up a puddle from an unexpected leak or giving a final polish to an exhibition case just before the doors opened. Numerous courses have been given for undergraduates and graduate students, without extra pay or compensatory time off. Almost every exhibition has represented an extra burden on the staff member or members, who selected the pieces shown, composed (and often typed) the labels and arranged the cases, and sometimes produced the text of a printed catalogue. No one can count the number of place cards for formal functions that were the single-handed work of Elli Garvey, who (usually in collaboration with Nancy Copeland) carefully laid out the seating arrangements and made the adjustments required by last-minute cancellations or the sudden appearance of unexpected guests, all so smoothly done that few realized the rapid improvisations that had taken place.

But these burdens had intangible compensations in the sense of community that they engendered and the shared fun that they produced. For the most part, people enjoyed their work and, what was more important, they enjoyed working together. As a result, they worked all the harder and more effectively. Much cataloguing of collections and searching of potential acquisitions was done out of hours, before nine A.M. when the library opened and long after five P.M. when it closed, or over weekends. But there were recreations as well. For many years Carolyn Jakeman saw to it that the anniversary of the formal dedication was properly celebrated with staff parties that became legendary: a buffet supper in the Reading Room was followed by games and square dancing in the Exhibition Room; in warmer weather, picnics and other *al fresco* parties were held at members' homes. Jackson set up the Collation Club, a luncheon group (no longer extant) at which many distinguished visitors were entertained; one summer, during his absence in England, the Club composed and printed the *Haughton Library Report,* a friendly burlesque of his annual *Houghton Library Report.* In more recent years, a mildly bacchanalian luncheon called the "Bonefeast" has been held for everyone between Christmas and New Year's Day. Celebrations of birthdays, retirements, honors and awards, and publication days happily punctuated the routine. But I must return to the events of 1942.

Pearl Harbor did nothing to simplify the problem of staging a suitable dedication, but it did not prevent the formal event from taking place with great *éclat* on February 28, 1942. The war in Europe and the Pacific lent a special significance to the occasion. Guests gathered in the Reading Room, where President James B. Conant introduced Arthur Houghton, who said that "The preservation of the records of scholarship and of truth will make it possible to bring forth a more enlightened civilization in the peace that will follow war. Harvard's great collections must be available to students of this country and of all nations"—sentiments that Mr. Conant then endorsed by stating that "It is our conception of the ancient duty of a company of scholars to cherish the creative spirit of mankind and treasure those things which the world will not willingly let die."[1]

Substantial gifts of books and manuscripts were then announced, and, to cap all, Professor Charles K. Webster of London University, on behalf of the British Ambassador, Lord Halifax, presented the *editio princeps* of the *Polycraticus* (Brussels, 1479–81?) of John of Salisbury. The assembled company then broke up for guided tours from top to bottom of the new building. It was the first of many notable occasions that have graced the library in the succeeding years, most of which are listed in the ensuing *Chronicle.*

The Houghton Library was designed with a capacity of about 250,000 volumes, and

---

1. A report of the dedication, with the full text of the remarks made on the occasion, may be found in *Harvard University Library Notes,* IV: 2 (March, 1942), 61-76.

when it opened it was approximately half full. Everyone felt that such a building would be a magnet to attract additional scholarly collections, but the size of the influx was unexpected and almost overwhelming. In its first year Jackson reported that some 9,600 printed books, 350 codices, and more than 42,000 autograph letters and documents had been added to its shelves: all the more remarkable because virtually all came as outright gifts or permanent deposits. This was the first of twenty-two annual reports of acquisitions written by Jackson and eagerly anticipated by the world of scholars, librarians, and booksellers. The series was continued by Jackson's successors through the acquisitions of the fiscal year 1976–77, when it halted because of budgetary constraints.

But the collections have steadily grown in size and strength, with or without annual reports, through gifts, acquisitions made with the income of restricted funds, and the systematic transfer of books deemed to be no longer safe on the open shelves of Widener and other libraries; indeed, such transfers will probably constitute much of its future expansion. Five years after its dedication, Houghton's stacks were already becoming crowded. Some relief was afforded when the Lamont Library opened in 1949. A whole floor of its underground stack was assigned to Houghton, but shelving was erected in only a third of this space (the east end, near Quincy Street), and much of that was taken up by the Theatre Collection. Only a few years later it was necessary to complete the installation of shelving. The Theatre Collection then moved to the west end of the Lamont stack and set up offices and a makeshift reading room there, releasing needed space for Houghton collections. Not until 1976 did the Theatre Collection have a proper reading room, offices, and stack space designed for it and built as part of the Pusey Library. By that time Houghton needed the space it had occupied, together with still more in Pusey to shelve its manuscripts. The shelving throughout its designated areas was carefully surveyed to make the most efficient use of it and allow for reasonable future expansion without undue moving of books and rearrangement of collections. As the Houghton Library reaches its fiftieth year, space for both staff and collections is again a problem to be faced.

The annual reports of acquisitions chronicle the high points of the growth of Houghton's scholarly collections and provide a more detailed history of them than is possible here. Many more particulars can be found in the meticulous records of accessions bound and shelved in the Reading Room, which reveal the source of each collection or individual item, the date acquired, and its donor or the dealer from whom it was purchased, its price, and the fund with which it was acquired. When a permanent shelf-mark has been assigned, it is entered in the accessions books. No more detailed records exist in any library approaching the size and scope of Houghton.

Acquisition is only one measure, and a rough one, of a library's growth. Accumulation is not enough; if books and manuscripts are not of high quality, adding to existing strengths, well and promptly catalogued, and freely available to scholars, the library cannot fulfill its proper function. Circulation in the Reading Room is a better gauge, though still rough. It has risen from approximately 17,000 items in 1942–43 to just under 174,000 in 1990–91, not including the nearly 8,000 items photographed on order, or the number of items used by the staff to answer reference questions or for their own research. In 1989–90 circulation reached

206,748 items, which compares very favorably with the 227,899 items fetched in the same period for readers in the Bodleian Library.[2]

What use is made of these books and manuscripts? It is possible to list only a few of the many substantial and authoritative works based in considerable part on Houghton collections by its staff, by its Harvard users, and by scholars all over the globe. Its many strengths made it the logical base for the revision of the *Short-Title Catalogue* by W. A. Jackson and F. S. Ferguson, recently brought to completion by Katharine F. Pantzer; for the compilation of the *Supplement* to Seymour de Ricci's *Census* of early manuscripts in the United States and Canada; and for the creation of Jacob Blanck's monumental *Bibliography of American Literature*, only now being brought to its conclusion by Michael Winship. In these, as in so many other works, the resources of the entire Harvard Library system provided support without which their completion would have been difficult if not impossible.

The Department of Printing and Graphic Arts alone provided the materials for Ruth Mortimer's four authoritative volumes on French and Italian illustrated books of the sixteenth century and Anne Anninger's companion volume of similar books from the Iberian peninsula, while the Curator Emerita, Eleanor Garvey, is proceeding with a like work on Italian illustrated books of the eighteenth century. The ensuing *Chronicle* records numerous exhibition catalogues, such as the one on *livres de peintre*, which have gained the status of works of reference. Forty years of manuscript cataloguing resulted in an eight-volume catalogue published by photo-offset from cards, making much of Houghton's manuscript collection more generally accessible, while the collections of printed works in certain areas (such as the works of Hugo von Hofmannsthal and the seventeenth-century French pamphlets known as *mazarinades*) produced standard bibliographies by photo-offset from catalogue cards. A work in progress, James Walsh's catalogue of incunabula throughout the Harvard library system, has already revealed much new and interesting information in its first published volume. This by no means exhausts the list of such works produced by members of the staff and their associates.

The collections of literary and historical documents constantly attract scholars engaged in producing biographical and critical works and editions in many fields. Their number and variety is too great to detail here, but their subjects range from the Dreyfus case and the writings of Leon Trotsky to the life and works of Emerson, Melville, Emily Dickinson, the James family, Keats, Tennyson, Carlyle, Goethe, Johnson, Boswell, the great writers of Russia, and many more. In all these endeavors the presence of a scholarly staff, ready and able to deal with the needs of its users, has been essential to the service it has been able to render to the world of learning. Without question the Houghton Library has more than lived up to the fondest hopes of those who planned it and built its collections over the past fifty years, and without question it will go on from strength to strength over the years to come.

WILLIAM H. BOND, *Librarian Emeritus*

---

2. *The Bodleian Library Record,* XIII: 6 (April, 1991), 460.

Houghton Library, ca. 1950.

The Houghton Library under construction, March 1941.
Harvard University News Office, courtesy Harvard University Archives.

Moving in, 1942. *Harvard University News Office, courtesy Harvard University Archives.*

1942

The Houghton Library opens on February 28, 1942. As the Rare Book Library of Harvard College, it incorporates the holdings of the old Widener Library Treasure Room, including the Department of Printing and Graphic Arts, founded by Philip Hofer in 1938. Provisions for shelving, insulation, air filtering and temperature and humidity control are all "state of the art." The aim is to duplicate those conditions "which have so perfectly preserved the libraries in English country houses and Tyrolian monasteries." The new building, designed by Perry, Shaw and Hepburn, is made possible by the generosity of Arthur A. Houghton, Jr., '29. William A. Jackson, William H. McCarthy, Jr., and Carolyn Jakeman spend a wild last night before opening for business chasing mice that have found their way in during construction.

Jackson offers English 186, a course on the problems and methods of bibliographical research and description, which he began to teach when he first came to Harvard in 1939 and will continue to teach until his death.

A series of exhibitions on such diverse subjects as Herman Melville, Chess, and Harvard in World War I is organized at the Harvard Club of New York.

Accessions for the year by gift, purchase, and permanent deposit total 9,600 printed books, 350 manuscript codices and over 42,000 autograph letters and documents, including Arthur A. Houghton's collection of books, manuscripts, drawings and memorabilia of John Keats, over 3000 illustrated books given by Philip Hofer, and William B. Osgood Field's huge collections of John Masefield, Rudyard Kipling and Edward Lear.

EXHIBITIONS

Exhibition Room

Accessions, 1942
Books from the William King Richardson Collection
The Bible, on the Occasion of the Centenary of the American Oriental Society
Military Books

LECTURES

Otto Benesch gives a series of three lectures on "Artistic and Intellectual Trends from Rubens to Daumier as Shown in Book Illustration" to the Friends of the Harvard Library during March and April.

PUBLICATIONS

The Reproduction Series of Harvard Library. Department of Printing and Graphic Arts, Harvard College Library, 1941 (No. 1: William Blake, *The Five Wise and the Five Foolish Virgins.* No. 2: Charles Schultz, *The Imperial Library in Vienna.* No. 3: *Avignon Letter of Indulgence.* XIV century French. No. 4: Albrecht Dürer, *The Four Horsemen of the Apocalypse.*)

Harvard Views: William Burgis, *A Prospect of the Colledges in Cambridge in New England,* 1726; D. Bell, *Cambridge Common from the Seat of Caleb Gannet, Esq. comprehending a view of Harvard University,* ca. 1805; Sam'l Farrar, *A Perspective View of the Episcopal Church (Christ Church) in Cambridge,* 1793; J. Abbot, *A North West View of Massachusetts Hall,* ca. 1798.

The Reminiscences of Sarah Kemble Siddons, 1773–1785. Edited, with a foreword by William Van Lennep. Cambridge: Widener Library, 1942.

William A. Jackson, *The Houghton Library, Harvard College.* Cambridge, 1942. A guide to the new building and its initial collections.

William A. Jackson, *The Houghton Library Report of Accessions for the Year 1941–42.* Cambridge, 1942.

An Autograph Letter of Ben Jonson to His Friend George Garrard. Cambridge, 1942. Houghton Library Brochure No. 1. Set and printed by members of the Houghton staff.

Byron on America: An Unpublished Letter to Dr. Joshua Henshaw Hayward, 19 March 1823. Cambridge, 1942. Houghton Library Brochure No. 2. Set and printed by members of the Houghton staff.

1943

The J. Harleston Parker Gold Medal for the best example of architecture in New England during 1942 is awarded to Perry, Shaw and Hepburn for the Houghton Library by the Boston Society of Architects at its annual meeting on May 4. Not only is Houghton acclaimed as a beautiful building; it is also considered to be fireproof, earthquake-proof, and capable of sustaining any enemy action short of a direct hit by a demolition bomb.

The Roosevelt Memorial Association presents its comprehensive collection of Theodore Roosevelt materials to the College Library; the manuscript portion of the collection is placed in Houghton.

The Bibliographical Society of America votes to sponsor a *Bibliography of American Literature (BAL)* and names a supervisory committee which includes William A. Jackson, Librarian of the Houghton Library. The project is supported by the Lilly Endowment, Inc. and its president, J. K. Lilly. *BAL* begins operations in New York in 1944 with Jacob Blanck as research director.

EXHIBITIONS

Exhibition Room

Renaissance Conference Exhibition
Calligraphy
Uncle Tom's Cabin
Alexander Pope
The De Tournes, 1542–1615, and *"Le Petit Bernard"*
Centennial Exhibition in Honor of Robert Southey, 1774–1843

PUBLICATIONS

William A. Jackson, *The Houghton Library Report of Accessions for the Year 1942–43.* Cambridge, 1943.
Kipling on the Japanese: An Unpublished Letter Written at the Time of the Russo-Japanese War to William Joshua Harding R.N., 2 September 1903. Cambridge, 1943. Houghton Library Brochure No. 3. Set and printed by members of the Houghton staff.
Otto Benesch, *Artistic and Intellectual Trends from Rubens to Daumier As Shown in Book Illustration.* Cambridge: Department of Printing and Graphic Arts, Harvard College Library, 1943.

1944

The most important acquisition of the year is the Gutenberg Bible presented to the Univer-

William Alexander Jackson.

sity on May 8, 1944 by George Widener, on behalf of his sister, Mrs. Widener Dixon. It is a perfect and complete copy of the first issue, on paper, of the first important book printed with moveable type. This great book, Harvard's greatest typographic treasure, is to be kept permanently in the Harry Elkins Widener Memorial Rooms. It soon becomes the object of countless pilgrimages by interested visitors.

William B. Osgood Field continues his munificence to the Library and deposits over 10,000 books and 3,000 prints and drawings. It is estimated that "it will take a long period to assimilate such a vast hoard." Field's Washington and Lafayette collections are exhibited at the Fogg Art Museum in the spring, and his unrivalled series of editions of "A Visit from St. Nicholas" is exhibited at Christmas at Houghton.

The papers of the American Board of Commissioners of Foreign Missions are deposited; occupying four double-faced stack ranges, they will remain Houghton's largest single archive.

William Inglis Morse is appointed Honorary Curator of Canadian History and Literature.

EXHIBITIONS

Exhibition Room

Clement C. Moore: "A Visit from St. Nicholas" (selected editions of the work, the recent gift of William B. Osgood Field)
Washington, Lafayette, Franklin
Polish exhibition
Six Centuries of Herbals
Albrecht Dürer Woodcuts
Max Beerbohm
William Penn

PUBLICATIONS

William A. Jackson, *The Houghton Library Report of Accessions for the Year 1943–44.* Cambridge, 1944.
William A. Jackson, *A Paper Read at the Presentation of the Gutenberg Bible.* Cambridge, 1944.
Thoreau's Pencils: An Unpublished Letter from Ralph Waldo Emerson to Caroline Sturgis, 19 May 1844. Cambridge, 1944. Houghton Library Brochure No. 4. Set and printed by members of the Houghton staff. All copies numbered with a pencil made by Thoreau and his brother.

1945

As the Second World War ends, William A.

Jackson laments the frightful destruction of books in battle and during the occupation, but is gratified that so many books have survived, in all likelihood to come on the market. He predicts that his will be the last generation to have the opportunity to accumulate important collections of the books of the distant past, and hopes that Harvard will have the wisdom and the means to take advantage of this opportunity.

A considerable number of manuscripts of modern European authors and statesmen are received during the year, including approximately one hundred letters by Stefan Zweig, the gift of Mrs. Gisella Selden-Goth.

Jackson makes a goodwill tour of South American libraries under the auspices of the State Department; meanwhile, there is a chance to acquire the entire remainder of Sir Thomas Phillipps's manuscripts, numbering some 12,000. Philip and Lionel Robinson, the London book dealers, who are negotiating with the trustees of the estate for their purchase, offer to turn them over to Harvard for a modest commission. Unfortunately, negotiations reach a crisis during Jackson's absence, and the collection is lost.

An exhibition of "Some *Christmas Carols* from Harvard College Library" is mounted at the Harvard Club of New York. An exhibition of nineteenth-century New England authors is on view at the Boston *Herald* Book Fair at Symphony Hall, Boston, October 15–18.

Friends of Morris H. Morgan for his widow establish the Morris H. Morgan Memorial for continuing his Persius collection, for the classics and rare books.

EXHIBITIONS

Exhibition Room

Lincolniana from the Collection of Clarence L. Hay
Illustrated Bird Books, Eighteenth to Twentieth Centuries
Milton's Poems, 1645–1945
An Exhibition of Fine Bindings, Twelfth to Eighteenth Centuries, Mainly from the Department of Printing and Graphic Arts
Tennyson: *Charge of the Light Brigade* and *Charge of the Heavy Brigade*
Ariosto (lifetime editions)

Ground Floor

European Capitals, a series of six exhibitions organized by the Department of Printing and Graphic Arts to celebrate the liberation of Europe. Individual exhibitions are devoted to London, Paris, Rome, Vienna, Leningrad and Moscow, and smaller capitals.

LECTURES

Edgar Wind, Seminar on the *Hypnerotomachia Poliphili.* Sponsored by the Department of Printing and Graphic Arts. April 24, 1945.

PUBLICATIONS

William A. Jackson, *The Houghton Library Report of Accessions for the Year 1944–45.* Cambridge, 1945.

Lawrence Wroth, *Some Reflections on the Book Arts in Early Mexico.* Cambridge: Department of Printing and Graphic Arts, Harvard College Library, 1945.

Elizabeth Mongan, Philip Hofer, and Jean Seznec, *Fragonard Drawings for Ariosto.* New York: Pantheon Books (for National Gallery of Art, Washington, D.C. and Harvard College Library, Cambridge, Massachusetts), 1945.

The Pre-Raphaelites: An Exhibition of Their Writings Supplementing the Fogg Exhibition of Their Paintings and Drawings

The Wonders of Nature, Mainly from Book Illustrations of the Eighteenth and Nineteenth Centuries (from the Department of Printing and Graphic Arts)

The Bible in the Vernacular, in Honor of the Publication of the New Revised Version of the New Testament

A Selection of Scandinavian Books

An Exhibition of Books Designed by Charles Ricketts, from the Collection of A. E. Gallatin

Rainer Maria Rilke, 1875–1926, an Exhibition in Commemoration of the Twentieth Anniversary of His Death. Part I: Original Works, in Manuscript and as Printed (continues in 1947).

Ground Floor

Complutensian Polyglot Bible

PUBLICATIONS

William A. Jackson, *The Houghton Library Report of Accessions for the Year 1945–46.* Cambridge, 1946.

Hogarth to His Wife, June 6, 1749. Cambridge, 1946. Set and printed by members of the Bibliography Seminar.

An Exhibition of Books Designed by Charles Ricketts from the Collection of A. E. Gallatin. [Cambridge]: The Houghton Library, Harvard University, 1946. Exhibition catalogue.

1946

Forty-six incunabula are added to the Houghton Library, fifteen of them the gift of Boies Penrose, '25. These include the *editiones principes* of Martial's *Epigrammata* [Venice, W. de Spira, 1470?], Pliny the Younger's *Panegyricus Trajano* [Milan, A. Zarotus, 1482], J. J. Pontanus's *De obedientia* (Naples, M. Moravus, 1490) and the Wodhull copy of Tibullus's *Elegiæ* (Reggio Emilia, 1481).

An exhibition of books and drawings by Randolph Caldecott from Houghton's Caroline Miller Parker Collection is mounted in the Ground Floor Hall of Widener.

William A. Jackson is nominated for the Presidency of the Bibliographical Society of America—of which he is not yet a member. He joins, is elected, and serves as president for two years.

EXHIBITIONS

Exhibition Room

Books and Manuscripts in Honor of the Fauré Festival
Modern French Illustrated Books from the Department of Printing and Graphic Arts

1947

On February 28, the fifth anniversary of the Library is celebrated with an exhibition of memorabilia ("Horrors" show).

Nearly twice as many readers are using the Houghton Library as were accommodated in the Widener Library Treasure Room before the war. The number of books and articles based on Houghton material shows a proportionate increase.

After thirty-one years in Widener Library, the office of the Theatre Collection moves to the ground floor of the Houghton Library. The collections remain in a segregated part of the Widener stacks, however, until the east end of the Houghton area of Lamont is ready to receive them in 1949. Theatre Collection books are available to readers through the Houghton Reading Room, the rest of the material by arrangement with the curator or his assistant.

William B. Wisdom deposits the papers of Thomas Wolfe in the Houghton Library. This vast array of books, letters and literary manu-

Reading Room Staff: Thomas Matthews, Mabel A.E. Steele, Mary K. Daehler, Carolyn Jakeman, and Harold M. Terrell.

scripts includes all "the little things, the big things, the secret things which show what a person really was" and record the life of one writer as completely as the life of any writer is ever likely to be recorded.

Volume I, Number 1 (Winter) of the *Harvard Library Bulletin* appears, edited in the Houghton Library by G. William Cottrell, Jr.; three issues per year are published. Publication continues through Volume XIV, Number 3 (Autumn 1960), when Cottrell retires. During this period, many of the contributors are members of the Houghton staff and many articles are based on Houghton collections.

A translation and partial reproduction of Giovanni Battista Verini's *Luminario* (Florence, 1527) is the first title in the Harvard-Newberry Library Calligraphic Studies. Ray Nash's *Dürer's 1511 Drawing of a Press* is printed by the Anthoensen Press in an edition of 550 with a collotype reproduction of the drawing executed by Meriden Gravure Company.

William Bentinck-Smith is appointed Honorary Curator of Type Specimens and Letter Design in the College Library. Arthur A. Houghton, Jr. is appointed Honorary Curator of the Keats Collection in the Houghton Library. Imrie de Vegh is appointed Honorary Curator of Eastern European History and Literature in the College Library.

EXHIBITIONS

Exhibition Room

Rainer Maria Rilke, 1875–1926
English Armorial Bindings
Chinese Shadow Figures (1642–1912) from the Collection of Theodore Bodde (under the auspices of the Theatre Collection)
Exhibition of Music (in conjunction with the Symposium on Music Criticism, May 1–3)

Baroque Book Illustrations and a Few Bindings of the Seventeenth Century (from the Department of Printing and Graphic Arts)

Keats Room

Manuscripts of Poems and Letters by John Keats Addressed to his Friends

Manuscripts and Pictures Relating to Keats's Illness, Journey to Italy, and Death in Rome

First Drafts and Other Manuscripts of Keats, Including Some Showing the Poet's Alterations and Corrections

Autograph Letters of John Keats Containing Drafts of Copies of his Poems

A Selection of Manuscripts of John Keats

Autograph Letters from the Correspondence of Taylor and Hessey, Keats's Publishers, Including a Number of Letters Recently Acquired

Miguel Cervantes: An Exhibition in Honor of the 400th Anniversary of his Birth

An Exhibition of Contemporary European Printing and Book Illustration (from the Department of Printing and Graphic Arts)

LECTURES

E. P. Goldschmidt, "The Spread of the Renaissance by Means of the Book." Part I (Type) January 9. Part II (Illustration) January 13. Part III (Ornament) January 16, 1947. Later published as *The Printed Book of the Renaissance* (1950).

PUBLICATIONS

William A. Jackson, *The Houghton Library Report of Accessions for the Year 1946–47.* Cambridge, 1947.

Luminario *or the Third Chapter of the* Liber Elementorum Litterarum. By Giovanni Baptista Verini in an English version by A. Johnson. Introduction by Stanley Morison. Cambridge: Harvard College Library; and Chicago: The Newberry Library, 1947.

The Ion of Plato. Translated by Benjamin Jowett. Cambridge: Harvard Printing Office and Department of Printing and Graphic Arts, 1947.

1948

The Manuscript Department is established as a separate entity under the curatorship of William H. Bond.

Two views of Harvard College by Jonathan Fisher, A.B. 1792, in the collection of the Boston Athenæum are published jointly by the Athenæum and the Department of Printing and Graphic Arts.

William H. McCarthy leaves to take up a position with the Rosenbach Company, New York.

Houghton stack area in Lamont, 1949.

Rosamond B. Loring is appointed Honorary Curator of the Paper Collection in the Department of Printing and Graphic Arts in the College Library.

EXHIBITIONS

Exhibition Room

An Exhibition of Contemporary European Printing and Book Illustration (continued from December 1947)

Thomas Wolfe: A Selection from the William B. Wisdom Collection and Other Sources

Odd Books: Books Unusual for Their Binding, Format, or Materials

Exhibition of Writings by and about Thomas Chatterton

A Century and a Half of Botanical Illustration: Color-Plate Books 1700–1850, Chiefly from the Department of Printing and Graphic Arts

An Exhibition in Honor of the Ninth Annual Liturgical Congress, Chiefly from the Department of Printing and Graphic Arts

An Exhibition of Sherlock Holmes, in Honor of the Collection of Harold Wilmerding Bell Deposited in the Harvard College Library by the Speckled Band of Boston

An Exhibition in Honor of the Charles Eliot Norton Lectures on "The Romantic Imagination" by Professor C. M. Bowra

Keats Room

Autograph Letters from the Correspondence of Taylor and Hessey (continued from December 1947)

Autograph Letters from Keats's Correspondence with Friends and Publishers Concerning His Work

Presentation Copies of Keats's Books

PUBLICATIONS

William A. Jackson, *The Houghton Library Report of Accessions for the Year 1947–48.* Cambridge, 1948.

Edgar Wind, *Bellini's Feast of the Gods, A Study in Venetian Humanism.* Cambridge: Harvard University Press (for Harvard College Library), 1948.

William Blake, *There is No Natural Religion.* Cambridge: Department of Printing and Graphic Arts, Harvard College Library, 1948.

Good Mrs. Smith: A Letter from Izaak Walton. Cambridge, 1948. Set and printed by members of the Bibliography Seminar.

1949

The collections of the Theatre Collection are moved from Widener 6 West to Lamont Basement East (see 1947), where they will remain until the opening of Pusey Library in 1976.

An exhibition of graphic processes is installed in Lamont Library by the Department of Printing and Graphic Arts. Collotype and offset exhibits are provided by Meriden Gravure Company.

Supported by a grant from the Harvard College Library, Jackson begins work on the revision of *A Short-Title Catalogue of Books Printed in England, Scotland & Ireland (STC).* This project is to continue uninterrupted for the next forty-five years.

The manuscripts and the *Nachlass* of Hugo von Hofmannsthal are deposited and given respectively by the poet's heirs (the manuscripts are to be withdrawn in 1964); Herbert Steiner serves as guest curator of the papers. The Karl Jacoby collection of books by von Hofmannsthal is acquired with funds provided by Gilbert H. Montague, '01.

Rosamond B. Loring establishes the Rosamond B. Loring Fund for her collection of Decorated Book Papers, which she will leave to the Department of Printing and Graphic Arts.

Mrs. Theodore Sheldon establishes the Edward Sheldon Memorial for the Harvard Theatre Collection in memory of her son, Class of '09.

EXHIBITIONS

Exhibition Room

Drawings for Book Illustration
Historic Design in Printing
Fielding and *Tom Jones*
Edgar Allan Poe
Don Quixote

Ground Floor

John Donne: The Editing of a Manuscript

PUBLICATIONS

William A. Jackson, *The Houghton Library Report of Accessions for the Year 1948–49.* Cambridge, 1949.

1950

The Houghton Library receives the Emily Dickinson Collection purchased for Harvard from Alfred Leete Hampson by Gilbert H. Montague, '01 and given "in happy memory" of his wife Amy Angell Collier Montague. Plans are made for a special room in which to display the collection, which includes the manuscripts

William King Richardson Room, ca. 1950.
Harvard University News Office, courtesy Harvard University Archives.

of over one thousand poems, nine hundred books from the Dickinson family library, oil portraits of Dickinson and her brother and sister and of her parents, her herbarium and the bureau in which she kept her manuscripts. Part of the collection that had been removed by Mabel Loomis Todd and never returned does not come to Houghton, having found its way eventually to Amherst College, a fact that gives rise to considerable discord between the two colleges. This controversy is finally resolved by a treaty. Harvard does not withdraw its claim to ownership of the Dickinson manuscripts at Amherst, but it agrees formally to let the matter drop. Other significant acquisitions during the year include Addison's draft essays for the *Spectator*, Masefield and Yeats manuscripts, a nearly

complete set of the Polish underground newspaper *Nowy Kurjer Warszawski*, 1939–44, and an additional sixty-two letters by Emily Dickinson, including twenty-six poems, presented by Mrs. Theodora V. W. Ward.

The *BAL* moves to a room on the second floor of the Houghton Library (see 1943) with Jacob Blanck in charge and Earle E. Coleman assisting.

During Jackson's absence in England, *The Haughton* [sic] *Library Report of Accessions for the Year 1949–50*, a burlesque of Jackson's annual reports, is issued by the Collation Club, an informal organization of male staff members, the cover device being drawn by Fernando Zóbel.

The Flora V. Livingston Bequest is established for the Rudyard Kipling Collection.

Exhibition Room

William Wordsworth, 1850–1950
Entomological Illustrations, 1400–1800
Emily Dickinson, 1830–1866
Manuscripts: Recent Acquisitions
Lettering and Calligraphy by Contemporary Artists
Four Hundred Years of Danish Literature
Natural Science 4 (Astronomy)
Bibliography/Catalogues

Ground Floor

Seventeenth-Century English Books on Christmas

PUBLICATIONS

William A. Jackson, *The Houghton Library Report of Accessions for the Year 1949–50.* Cambridge, 1950.
A Letter Written in Contemplation of Death by John Wilmot, Earl of Rochester. Cambridge, 1950. Set and printed by members of the Bibliography Seminar. Linoleum cut by Fernando Zóbel. A few of the copies were printed in white ink on black paper.

1951

The great event of the year is the bequest of the library of William King Richardson, 1880, which is placed on display in the room which he provided for it on the top floor of the Library. This bequest greatly strengthens the Harvard collection of illuminated manuscripts, first editions of the classics, and fine bindings of the sixteenth to nineteenth centuries. Among the illuminated manuscripts are at least half a dozen which would rank, in any company, in the first class of their type and period.

The Harvard collection of T. S. Eliot, '10, which for several years was on deposit in Eliot House, is placed permanently in the Houghton Library. This collection includes manuscripts, periodicals, translations, memorabilia and juvenilia, together with first and later editions of the separate works. The collection was originally assembled by the author's brother, the late Henry Ware Eliot, '02 and is derived in part from family holdings.

Several other manuscripts of considerable importance are also acquired, including an Italian tenth-century Horace, presented by Stephen W. Phillips, '95, a grant of lands to the Gilbertine monks, dated September 7, 1199, the gift of Mr. and Mrs. Donald F. Hyde, and a twelfth-century text of the medieval *Ganymed and Helena.* A final group of American and British drawings for book illustration is received from the bequest of William B. Osgood Field.

The Rosamond B. Loring Collection of Decorated Book Papers is received by the Department of Printing and Graphic Arts.

Dard Hunter is appointed Honorary Curator of Paper-Making and Allied Arts in the Department of Printing and Graphic Arts in the College Library.

EXHIBITIONS

Exhibition Room

Lafcadio Hearn
Melville: Celebrating the Centenary of *Moby Dick*
Max Beerbohm
Prince Igor's Raid: Exhibition Arranged for the Visiting Committee of the Slavic Department

PUBLICATIONS

William A. Jackson, *The Houghton Library Report of Accessions for the Year 1950–51.* Cambridge, 1951.
William A. Jackson, *A General Note of the Prices of Binding all Sorts of Books.* Cambridge, 1951. Facsimile with preface, published as a keepsake for a meeting of the Bibliographical Society of America.

Jacob Blanck in the *BAL* Room, ca. 1963.

[William H. Bond], *Studies in Library Œconomy in Honor of Fernando Zóbel-Montojo.* Cambridge, 1951. Parodies of English verse converted to library subjects.

William H. Bond, ed., *The Development of Knowledge of the Blood.* Cambridge, 1951. Exhibition catalogue.

Philip Hofer, *Baroque Book Illustration: A Short Survey From the Collection in the Department of Printing and Graphic Arts, Harvard College Library.* Cambridge: Harvard University Press, 1951.

Charles Nodier, *The Book Collector.* Foreword by Philip Hofer. Cambridge, 1951.

The Reading Room looks on the Bridge;
The Bridge, in turn, looks on the Yard;
And musing there one hour alone
I thought of many an index card
Shot arrow-like from Mezzanine, O
Paradox worthy of a Zeno.

❧ ❧ ❧

— [W.H.B.], in *Studies in Library Œconomy*

Visitors at the Manuscript Exhibition, 1955.
Harvard University News Office, courtesy Harvard University Archives.

Old Theatre Collection Rooms on Houghton ground floor, ca. 1952.
Harvard University News Office, courtesy Harvard University Archives.

1952

The tenth anniversary of the library is celebrated with a folkdance.

New exhibition rooms for the Theatre Collection, given by Mrs. Theodore Sheldon of Chicago in memory of her son Edward Brewster Sheldon, '08, open in November. The three decorative rooms are at the foot of the stairs on the ground floor of the Houghton Library, in space previously used for shelving books. One of the rooms is named for George Chaffee. A permanent exhibition of theatrical material is installed.

William A. Jackson and Philip Hofer together offer English 191hf, a survey of the history of the book, including an introduction to elementary bibliography, intended primarily for those students who are or wish to become book collectors.

William H. Bond receives a Fulbright Fellowship to serve for a year as Assistant Keeper in the Manuscript Department of the British Museum. He returns in the summer of 1953.

In October, the Gray Herbarium places approximately 330 pre-Linnaean botanical books on deposit in the Houghton Library, where they join similar collections from the Arnold Arboretum and the Museum of Comparative Zoology deposited in 1948 and 1949.

Major acquisitions include the Bayard L. Kilgour Collection of Russian Literature, the Augustin H. Parker Collection of Oliver Goldsmith, and the Rosamond B. Loring Collection of Decorated Papers.

The Rosamond B. Loring Fund is augmented by a bequest under the will of Augustus P. Loring, Jr., '08, the husband of the donor. Friends establish the Houghton Library Development Fund. Augustin H. Parker, 1897 establishes the Augustin H. Parker Bequest for his collection of Oliver Goldsmith.

EXHIBITIONS

Exhibition Room

William Pickering: Publisher and Bookseller, 1796–1854
Baroque Book Illustration
Books and Manuscripts from the Library of William King Richardson
Islamic Manuscripts and Miniatures

The Works of Victor Hugo Commemorating the 150th Anniversary of His Birth
A Choice of Autographs from the Harvard Collections Assembled in Honor of the National Society of Autograph Collectors
Renaissance Science, an Exhibition for the New England Conference on Renaissance Studies

Keats Room

Letters and Poems of John Keats Written in the Spring of 1819
Manuscripts, Drawings and Association Items by or relating to Keats and Members of his Circle, Recently Acquired
Selected Autograph Manuscripts of John Keats

Ground Floor

Japanese Bird Scrolls
Elizabeth Barrett Browning: *Casa Guidi Windows* (1851)
Roland Fréart de Chambray, *Parallèle de l'architecture antique avec la moderne* (1650)
Abraham Lincoln: Autograph Manuscript of the Baltimore Address, October 19, 1864
Samuel Francis Smith: Autograph Manuscripts of "America" and its First Printing in Boston, 1831

Printing and Graphic Arts Room

Mediæval Illuminated Manuscripts
Levaillant, *Histoire naturelle des oiseaux de paradis*, 1806, and Audebert, *Histoire naturelle des singes*, 1799
Recent Accessions
Islamic Manuscripts
Palace Construction in Eighteenth-Century Vienna

PUBLICATIONS

William A. Jackson, *The Houghton Library Report of Accessions for the Year 1951–52.* Cambridge, 1952.
Rosamond B. Loring, *Decorated Book Papers, Being an Account of Their Designs and Fashions.* Cambridge: Harvard University Press, 1952.
Absalon Preserved: A Letter from John Dryden to Dr. Richard Busby. Cambridge, 1952. Set and printed by members of the Bibliography Seminar.

1953

The most important acquisition of the year in the field of twentieth-century continental literature is the Rainer Maria Rilke Collection, which was formed by the late Professor Richard von Mises. It is the first important acquisition made possible by the recent receipt of income from the trust established by Amy Lowell. The collection consists of several hundred printed items—including every book Rilke ever wrote—nearly four hundred letters, photographs, drawings and sketches of Rilke made at various periods of his life, and an oil portrait by Leonid Pasternak.

Additional shelving is added to the basement level of Lamont to provide additional stack space for the Houghton Library. This space was originally assigned to Houghton when Lamont Library opened in January 1949, but at that time it received only forty percent of its potential complement of shelves.

A "radio play," "Subversion in the Houghton Library," is written and tape-recorded by William M. Howie for Houghton's eleventh birthday on February 28. Various staff members, including William A. Jackson and Philip Hofer, play themselves in this take-off on the McCarthy hearings.

Philip Hofer, '21 establishes the Department of Printing and Graphic Arts Art Reserve Fund for the publication and care of prints and drawings and the Department of Printing and Graphic Arts Book Reserve Fund for the publication and care of books. Mrs. Theodore Sheldon establishes the Edward Sheldon Book Fund (see 1949). By residuary bequest William Inglis Morse establishes in memory of his wife, the Susan A. E. Morse Fund for acquisitions with preference for Canadiana; part of the income is made available to the Houghton Library.

EXHIBITIONS

Exhibition Room

A Choice of Autographs from Harvard Collections
An Exhibition on the Occasion of the Convention of the Episcopal Church
Books and Manuscripts Honoring the One-Hundredth Anniversary of the Publication of Uncle Tom's Cabin by Harriet Beecher Stowe
William Pickering
An Exhibition of Literary Books and Manuscripts in Honor of the Modern Languages Association
Mathematical Books and Manuscripts
An Exhibition Commemorating the 150th Anniversary of the Birth of Ralph Waldo Emerson (1803–1953)
Tercentenary Exhibition in Honor of the First Publication of Izaak Walton's Compleat Angler (1653–1953)

Keats Room

Selected Autograph Manuscripts of John Keats
Letters of Keats (Autographs and Transcripts) and of Members of the Keats Circle, July 1820 to May 1821

Selected Autograph Letters of John Keats, Containing Drafts or Copies of His Poems
Selected Manuscripts of John Keats

Ground Floor

Rabelais

PUBLICATIONS

William A. Jackson, *The Houghton Library Report of Accessions for the Year 1952–53.* Cambridge, 1953.
A.N.L. Munby, *Floreat Bibliomania.* Cambridge, England: Rampant Lions Press (by Will Carter for Philip Hofer), 1953.
Philip Hofer, *An Illustration by William Blake for the 'Circle of the Traitors, Dante's* Inferno *Canto XXXII.* Meriden, Conn.: Meriden Gravure Co., 1953.

1954

Acquisitions include a complete series of first editions of Ivan Cankar (then considered the foremost Serbian novelist), a copy of Picasso's *Eaux-fortes originales pour des textes de Buffon* (Paris, 1942), an unrecorded file of *Naprea*, a military newspaper published by Serbian troops during World War I, and nine letters of Mata Hari and one of Edith Cavell, the latter items the gifts of James N. B. Hill, '15. The most distinguished additions to the Theatre Collection are twenty-eight magnificent watercolor designs by Natalia Goncharova for the costumes and decor of Diaghilev's famous 1914 production of *Le coq d'or.*

Philip Hofer delivers Lowell Lectures at the Museum of Fine Arts on "The Prints of Francisco Goya y Lucientes."

The "Houghton Movie," featuring staff members and the ghosts of Thomas Hollis, John Donne and Walt Whitman, is filmed for the Library's twelfth birthday.

EXHIBITIONS

Exhibition Room

Edward Lear (1812–1888): First Editions and Original Drawings
An Exhibition of Architectural Books (with M.I.T.)
An Exhibition of Color in Printing and Illustration
An Exhibition of Recent Accessions in Honor of the Class of 1929
A Victorian Illustrator: The Harvard Field-Collection of John Leech
An Exhibition of Bestiaries and Fables

Keats Room

Selected Manuscripts of John Keats (throughout)

Ground Floor

Drawings of Coffee Pots by Count Rumford

Randolph Caldecott's Illustrations for Hallam Tennyson's "Jack and the Beanstalk"

A Group of Bindings from the Aeronautical Collection of William A. M. Burden, '27, Recently Deposited in the Houghton Library

Printing and Graphic Arts Room

Color in Printing and Illustration: Color Reproduction of Manuscripts

PUBLICATIONS

William A. Jackson, *The Houghton Library Report of Accessions for the Year 1953–54.* Cambridge, 1954.

Edmund Waller to John Evelyn. Cambridge, 1954. Set and printed by members of the Bibliography Seminar.

A Bestiary by Toulouse-Lautrec. Prepared by the Department of Printing and Graphic Arts, Harvard Library. Introduction by Philip Hofer. Fogg Museum Picture Book Number 3. Cambridge: Fogg Art Museum and Harvard College Library, 1954.

Edward Lear, *Drawing Book Alphabet.* Cambridge: Harvard College Library, 1954.

The First Writing Book, An English Translation and Facsimile Text of Arrighi's Operina, *The First Manual of the Chancery Hand.* Introduction and notes by John Howard Benson. No. 2 in the Studies in the History of Calligraphy. New York: Chiswick Book Shop; and New Haven: Yale University Press, 1954.

1955

A major exhibition of a selection of Harvard's illuminated and calligraphic manuscripts with a substantial catalogue by William H. Bond and Philip Hofer is held in the Fogg Art Museum and the Houghton Library from February 14 through April 1.

A second major exhibition devoted to Harvard Stage Designers Lee Simonsen, Robert Edmond Jones and Donald Oenslager is held at the Fogg Art Museum. Theatre Collection curator William Van Lennep meets Helen Willard, then working at the Fogg, who assists with the exhibition.

The bulk of the William Bentinck-Smith Typographical Collection is deposited in the Department of Printing and Graphic Arts.

Volume I of the *BAL* (Henry Adams to Donn Byrne) is published by Yale University Press in November.

EXHIBITIONS

Exhibition Room

An Exhibition in Honor of Robert Frost in His Eightieth Year: Rare Editions, Manuscripts, and Association Items

The Archæological Institute of America

An Exhibition of Illuminated and Calligraphic Manuscripts

Books by Undergraduates

Books and Manuscripts by T. S. Eliot

Keats Room

Selected Manuscripts of John Keats (throughout)

Ground Floor

Nathaniel Hawthorne, 1804–1864: The 150th Anniversary of His Birth

Words and Names

An Exhibition of Illuminated and Calligraphic Manuscripts

Printing and Graphic Arts Room

Modern Calligraphy

Mabel Steele and students in the Keats Room, 1955. *Harvard University News Office, courtesy Harvard University Archives.*

PUBLICATIONS

William A. Jackson, *The Houghton Library Report of Accessions for the Year 1954–55.* Cambridge, 1955.

T. S. Eliot at T. S. Eliot Exhibition, 1955.
Photo by Charles McCormick, courtesy of The Boston Globe.

[William H. Bond and Philip Hofer], *Illuminated and Calligraphic Manuscripts.* Cambridge: Harvard College, 1955. Exhibition catalogue.
A Letter from Glanvill to More. Cambridge, 1955. Set and printed by members of the Bibliography Seminar.

1956

During an administrative reorganization of the College Library, the title of the head of the Houghton Library is changed from "Assistant Librarian of the College Library in charge of the Houghton Library" to "Librarian of the Houghton Library in the Harvard College Library."

English 191hf, the Study of Fine Books, is once more offered to would-be book collectors by William A. Jackson and Philip Hofer (see 1952).

Acquisitions include Albert Einstein's inaugural dissertation for the Ph.D. at the University of Zürich, an inscribed copy of André Gide's first book (all copies of which he attempted to destroy), one of seventy-five copies of Marcel Proust's *Du côté de chez Grasset* (Paris, 1927) and the René Gaffé copy of *La révolution surréaliste* (Paris, 1924–27), on large paper, bound by Paul Bonet and accompanied by letters and printed documents pertaining to the movement.

The Department of Printing and Graphic Arts issues a reproduction of *A N.W. View of Hollis, Harvard and Massachusetts Halls* painted in watercolor by Joseph Story in 1795 as part of its series of historic Harvard and Cambridge views.

The residuary bequest of Carl T. Keller, '94

establishes the Keller Fund, part of which is made available to the Houghton Library.

EXHIBITIONS

Exhibition Room

English Architectural Books of the Seventeenth and Eighteenth Centuries
The Heine Collection at Harvard
Armenian exhibition
Recent Accessions
Elizabeth Barrett Browning
Exhibition of Printed and Manuscript Music in Honor of the Opening of the Eda Kuhn Music Library

Printing and Graphic Arts Room

John Martin, 1789–1854

PUBLICATIONS

William A. Jackson, *The Houghton Library Report of Accessions for the Year 1955–56.* Cambridge, 1956.
ABC Book Designed by Willi Harwerth. Offenbach-am-Main, January, 1933. Cambridge: Department of Printing and Graphic Arts, The Houghton Library, 1956.

A Visit to Rome in 1764. Fogg Museum Picture Book Number 5. Cambridge: Fogg Art Museum and Harvard College Library, 1956.
A Letter from White of Selborne. Cambridge, 1956. Set and printed by members of the Bibliography Seminar.

1957

A grant from the Ford Foundation, channeled via the American Council of Learned Societies, makes it possible for Jackson to enlarge his collection of reference materials for the *STC* and to hire extra assistants to speed work on the revision.

Major acquisitions include the Lee M. Friedman Collection of Judaica and a large miscellaneous collection from an anonymous donor, containing many *entrée* and *fête* books of all periods, an even larger number of remarkable bindings, and a number of manuscripts and letters of importance.

Jackson and his staff, ca. 1955.

William Bentinck-Smith, '37, Assistant to the President and Honorary Curator of Type Specimens and Letter Design in the Department of Printing and Graphic Arts, gives a lecture entitled "Some Type Founders and Their Work" before the Society of Printers in the Exhibition Room of the Houghton Library. This lecture draws its material almost entirely from Bentinck-Smith's own collection of type-specimen books on deposit in Houghton (see 1955).

Volume II of the *BAL* (George W. Cable to Timothy Dwight) is published in December.

Osgood Hooker, '21 gives a fund to be used for the purchase of books for the Department of Printing and Graphic Arts. William Bentinck-Smith, '37 establishes the Bentinck-Smith Fund for the support of his typographical collection in the Department of Printing and Graphic Arts.

EXHIBITIONS

Exhibition Room

Manuscripts and First Editions of Henry Wadsworth Longfellow to Commemorate the 150th Anniversary of His Birth
Books from the Libraries of the Kings and Queens of England
Drawings and Lithographs by Thomas Shotter Boys, 1803–1874
Illustrated Books of William Blake

Keats Room

Portraits of Keats Used as Frontispieces in Editions of His Works

Ground Floor

Books Dedicated to Elizabeth Barrett Browning
Elizabethan and Jacobean Manuscripts Recently Received

Printing and Graphic Arts Room

Baroque Vienna
London As It Is, by Thomas Shotter Boys: Drawings and Prints

PUBLICATIONS

William A. Jackson, *The Houghton Library Report of Accessions for the Year 1956–57*. Cambridge, 1957.

1958

A special map room for Houghton's holdings of sheet maps and atlases (including the great Hauslab-Prince Liechtenstein Collection of Early Maps and the Bagrow Collection of Russian Maps) is constructed at the west end of Houghton beneath Lamont Library and is fitted out with cases from the Geographical Institute.

James E. Walsh, Head of the Department of Rare Book Cataloguing, receives a Fulbright Fellowship to aid in the preparation of a biography and bibliography of Johannes Sambucus, Hungarian humanist and historian of the sixteenth century.

William A. Jackson receives the gold medal of the Stationers' Company, London.

Philip Hofer, '21 establishes the Hofer Fund for the Department of Printing and Graphic Arts. George S. Mumford, '25 and Mrs. Sydney P. Clark establish the George S. Mumford, 1887 Book Fund in memory of their father. The Sarah Norton Bequest is established to buy rare books for the Charles Eliot Norton Collection. The Harry Elkins Widener Collection Endowment is established by the trust created by Eleanore Elkins Rice (formerly Eleanore Elkins Widener) for the curatorship, care of the collection, and maintenance of the rooms.

EXHIBITIONS

Exhibition Room

Books and Manuscripts of Interest in the History of Philosophy
An Exhibition to Commemorate the 2,000th Anniversary of the Birth of Ovid on March 20, 43 B.C.: A Selection of Early Printed Editions, Illustrated Editions, and Drawings
A Selection of Books and Manuscripts from a Recent Gift to the Harvard Library
A Selection of Books from the Deposit of Susan Bliss
The Paris of Henry of Navarre

Keats Room

Selected Manuscripts of John Keats
Keats and the Theatre (including playbills from the Theatre Collection)

Ground Floor

A Manuscript Alphabet by Veronica Ruzicka
Early Issues of *Uncle Tom's Cabin*

Printing and Graphic Arts Room

Illustrated Books of William Blake
Flower Books
Modern Color Printing
Chinese Scrolls

PUBLICATIONS

William A. Jackson, *The Houghton Library Report of Accessions for the Year 1957–58*. Cambridge, 1958.

Two Letters from Isaac Watts to Thomas Foxcroft. Cambridge, 1958. Set and printed by the Bibliography Seminar.

1959

The Pope Orrery, refurbished by David P. Wheatland, '22 is installed in the Ground Floor hall.

The Houghton Library is described and depicted in a *Life* magazine article on the Harvard Libraries, "Storehouse for Scholarship," on March 9.

Acquisitions include books and manuscripts by modern authors including Theodore Dreiser, Richard Watson Gilder and Marianne Moore. Jackson laments the fact that as the market prices of modern authors approach those of classic authors, collecting becomes an ever greater gamble. He suggests that Harvard men consider collecting "the original editions of the authors they believe will be important in the year 2500" so that they may be made available to future scholars.

Volume III of the *BAL* (Edward Eggleston to Bret Harte) is published in October.

The Bayard L. Kilgour, Jr., '27 Fund for Russian Belles-Lettres is established. William S. Spaulding, '37 establishes the William S. Spaulding Fund for processing and repairing his gift of books and for the Houghton Library.

EXHIBITIONS

Exhibition Room

The Grand Tour: An Exhibition of Eighteenth-Century Views

Italian Books and Manuscripts Exhibited in the honor of the Marchesa Origo

The Paris of Henry of Navarre: Books and Manuscripts Illustrative of the Book [by Nancy Roelker] of That Title Published by the Harvard University Press

Maps of Siberia and Russia

Books Purchased with the Fund Established by Henry Saltonstall Howe, Class of 1869

An Exhibition Honoring the Centennial of *On the Origin of Species*

William Makepeace Thackeray: Based upon the Collection Formed and Presented by Herbert L. Carlebach, '09 (continues into 1960)

Keats Room

Keats and the Theater

In Commemoration of the Centenary of the Death of Leigh Hunt (1784–1850)

Ground Floor

The Original Manuscript and First Printings of "America," on the 150th Anniversary of the Birth of Samuel Francis Smith

200th Anniversary of the Birth of Robert Burns, January 25, 1759

A Selection from Harvard's Books of Hours

Early Books on Astronomy to Signalize the Installation of the Pope Orrery

Printing and Graphic Arts Room

Chinese Scrolls

Persian Miniatures

PUBLICATIONS

William A. Jackson, *The Houghton Library Report of Accessions for the Year 1958–59*. Cambridge, 1959.

Ray Nash, *American Writing Masters and Copybooks, History and Bibliography Through Colonial Times.* No. 3 in the Studies in the History of Calligraphy series. Cambridge: Harvard College Library and Chicago, The Newberry Library, 1959.

William B. Todd, *The Kilgour Collection of Russian Literature, 1750–1920. With Notes on Early Books and Manuscripts of the 16th and 17th Centuries.* Preface by William A. Jackson. Cambridge: Harvard University Press (for Harvard College Library), 1959.

1960

Helen Willard is named Curator of the Theatre Collection upon the retirement of William Van Lennep. Van Lennep retains an office in Lamont basement until his death in 1962.

Mrs. Henry James of New York bequeaths to Harvard the books in her possession which relate to Henry James, Sr., Henry James the novelist, and Professor William James. In past years, her husband and other members of the family have given Harvard many volumes associated with these three. Other acquisitions include the bookplate collection of Winward Prescott, '09, bequeathed by his daughter, Mrs. Elizabeth Prescott Morgan. Bookplates by modern artists such as Daniel Chester French and Félicien Rops are especially well-represented.

The Reading Room continues to be used ever more heavily. In one month during the summer, 9500 books and manuscripts are recorded at the Reading Room desk as having been used by scholars. This was a large number and meant that not only was the room crowded—extra chairs had to be brought in—but the fetching and returning of so many items was a considerable chore. Jackson is concerned about the heavy use of modern collections of manuscripts, where the paper is often of the poorest quality and inevitably doomed to decay. He stresses the need for preservation funds.

Frederick M. Dearborn, '33 establishes the Frederick M. Dearborn Bequest for the support of his Collection of Political and Military Americana.

EXHIBITIONS

Exhibition Room

William Makepeace Thackeray: Based upon the Collection Formed and Presented by Herbert L. Carlebach, '09

Pierre de Ronsard, *Prince des Poètes Français*
Isaac Sprague (1811–1895), Artist and Naturalist
Paul Verlaine (1844–1896): Books and Manuscripts
Sixteenth-Century Spanish and Portuguese Book Illustration

Keats Room

A Selection from the Manuscripts of Keats and His Circle Acquired in the Years 1950–1959
Selected Manuscripts and Marginalia of John Keats

Ground Floor

Magna Charta: A Special Copy Printed in Gold on Vellum by Charles Whittingham, 1815
Manuscripts of Sir William Herschel

Printing and Graphic Arts Room

Persian Miniatures
Early Printed Fables and Bestiaries

PUBLICATIONS

William A. Jackson, *The Houghton Library Report of Accessions for the Year 1959–60.* Cambridge, 1960.

Helen Willard and Edwin Binney, 3rd, 1966.

Old Emily Dickinson Room, ca. 1959.
Harvard University News Office, courtesy Harvard University Archives.

Wars & Rumors of Wars: A Foreshadowing of the Invincible Armada. Cambridge, 1960. Set and printed by the Bibliography Seminar. Linoleum cut by Fernando Zóbel.
Marie Angel, *A Bestiary.* Cambridge, 1960.
Jules Renard, *Natural History.* Lithographs by Walter Stein. Edited and translated by Philip Hofer. New York: Walker and Co., 1960.

1961

A major exhibition at the Museum of Fine Arts, Boston, devoted to the development of the *livre d'artiste* in Western Europe and the United States, is organized by Philip Hofer and the Department of Printing and Graphic Arts and includes many items from the Library's collections. The catalogue by Eleanor M. Garvey soon becomes a classic reference work in the field.

Scores of additions are made to the Russian literature collection by Bayard L. Kilgour, Jr., '27, including a dozen firsts of Gorky in the original wrappers, three of Pasternak, and three of Tolstoy.

Robert Frost, '01, gives the complete dossier regarding his participation in the inauguration of President John F. Kennedy, '40. Several other additions to the Frost collection are made by David McCord, who also gives some of his own manuscripts and ephemera.

William B. Wisdom answers Jackson's appeal for help with the preservation of materials on cheap wood-pulp paper with a generous donation. The Thomas Wolfe Collection, which Wisdom has brought together at Harvard over many years, contains thousands of sheets of manuscript on the cheapest of yellow scratch-paper.

At this point a little money from the Houghton Development Fund, raised by Jackson and Hofer, begins to be available on a regular basis for the support of publications. This will be used to support many catalogues during the next thirty years.

The Amy Angell Collier Montague and Gilbert H. Montague, '01 Fund is established; part is designated for the maintenance of the Houghton Library.

EXHIBITIONS

Exhibition Room

Exhibition of Sparks MS 49
An Exhibition of Books Published When They Were 21 or Younger by One Hundred Authors Who Later Became Famous
Francis Bacon 300th Anniversary
Ariosto

PUBLICATIONS

William A. Jackson, *The Houghton Library Report of Accessions for the Year 1960–61.* Cambridge, 1961.

William A. Jackson, *An Exhibition of Books Published When They Were 21 or Younger by One Hundred Authors Who Later Became Famous.* Cambridge, 1961.

Increase Mather, *The Young Minister's Preservative.* Cambridge, 1961. Set and printed by members of the Bibliography Seminar.

Eleanor M. Garvey, *The Artist and the Book, 1860–1960 in Western Europe and the United States.* Introduction by Philip Hofer. Cambridge: Department of Printing and Graphic Arts, Harvard College Library; and Boston: The Museum of Fine Arts, 1961. Catalogue of an exhibition at the Museum of Fine Arts, Boston.

Linoleum cut by Katharine F. Pantzer.

THE THIRD DECADE: 1962–1971

Harry Elkins Widener Memorial Rooms.
Photo by Diane Asséo Griliches.

William A. Jackson and Thomas Matthews at Matthews's retirement party, 1963.

1962

While users come in ever increasing numbers, the Library is having difficulty finding new cataloguers competent to record new acquisitions and the backlog of former accessions. "Not everyone has the temperament to make a good cataloguer," Jackson notes in his annual report. "Accuracy and some linguistic competence are pre-requisites, but equally important is the ability to undertake what some might call drudgery for the sake of the satisfaction of making orderly records of books and manuscripts, most of which, to such a person, are a joy to behold."

William H. Bond and S. U. Faye's *Supplement to the Census of Medieval and Renaissance Manuscripts in the United States and Canada* is published by the Bibliographical Society of America.

William Bentinck-Smith, '37 presents his collection of type-specimen books to the Department of Printing and Graphic Arts, together with a fund for further acquisitions (see 1955).

William A. Jackson receives an honorary degree, L.H.D., from Harvard. His citation acclaims him as the University's "Great Acquisitor" for doubling or trebling Harvard's rare book and manuscript holdings in quality as well as in quantity.

On October 18, the semiannual meeting of the Bibliographical Society of America is held at Lamont Library, preceded by sherry at the Houghton Library, where members and guests view "Bibliotheca Chimærica," an exhibition of catalogues of imaginary books.

William Van Lennep, Curator of the Theatre Collection from 1940-60, dies. Van Lennep was responsible for many major acquisitions during his twenty-year curatorship and was an active member of the faculty, teaching Comp Lit 283. He also spent many years working on volume I of *The History of the London Stage, 1660-1700*, which was published posthumously.

Mrs. Hugh Gray Lieber gives the Hugh Gray Lieber Fund to the Department of Printing and Graphic Arts for the Department's general endowment and to support the Lieber Collection of drawings and manuscripts. The William B. Wisdom Book and Manuscript Preservation Fund is established by gift of the Fidelis Foundation.

Exhibition Room
Italy in the Eighteenth Century: Illustrated Books
Reisinger Exhibition
Bibliotheca Chimærica

Roger E. Stoddard, "C. Fiske Harris: Collector of American Poetry and Plays." For a meeting of the Bibliographical Society of America, October 18, 1962. Later printed in *PBSA*.

William A. Jackson, *The Houghton Library Report of Accessions for the Year 1961-62*. Cambridge, 1962.
William A. Jackson, *Bibliotheca Chimærica: A Catalogue of an Exhibition of Catalogues of Imaginary Books*. Cambridge, 1962.
Thomas Goffe, *A Songe Ascribed to Thomas Goffe*. Cambridge, 1962. Set and printed by the Bibliography Seminar. Linoleum cut on wrapper by Katharine F. Pantzer.
Zeph Stewart, ed., *Selections from Horace: Readings of an Unpublished Tenth-Century Manuscript in the Harvard University Library*. Cambridge: Adams House Printers, 1962.

1963

Rodney G. Dennis, III joins Houghton staff as a cataloguer in the Manuscript Department.

Philip Hofer receives the honorary degree of D.F.A. from Bates College.

Volume IV of the *BAL* (Nathaniel Hawthorne to Joseph Holt Ingraham) is published in June.

Thomas Matthews retires after 22 years. Matthews, who was born in Wales and served in the British army during the Boer War and World War I, came to the United States in 1921 and was a butler for many years in many of the North Shore's wealthiest homes before coming to the Houghton Library, where he brought dignity, efficiency, and old-world courtliness to his position as front desk guard.

Harrison D. Horblit is appointed Honorary Curator of the History of Science in the College Library. Curt H. Reisinger is appointed Honorary Curator of the Slavic Collections in the College Library.

The gift of Mrs. Frank G. Wendt is used to establish the Charles Knowles Fund, to be used for the encouragement of young people in the field of printing and graphic arts.

EXHIBITIONS

Exhibition Room

The History of the Medieval Book in Western Europe: Some Examples from the Collections at Harvard
Manuscripts Acquired Since 1938
T. S. Eliot: 75th Birthday Exhibition
History of Medicine

PUBLICATIONS

William A. Jackson, *The Houghton Library Report of Accessions for the Year 1962–63.* Cambridge, 1963.
A Letter of Herschel. Cambridge, 1963. Set and printed by members of the Bibliography Seminar.
Marie Angel, *A New Bestiary.* Cambridge, 1963.
Edward Lear, *Flora Nonsensica.* Foreword by Philip Hofer. Cambridge: Department of Printing and Graphic Arts, Harvard College Library, 1963.

1964

The Houghton Library loses its first Librarian, an imposing figure who set its course and shaped its policies. William A. Jackson dies on October 18. The guidelines that Jackson laid out for the Houghton Library include "a tradition of flexibility to take advantage of emergent opportunities and to meet changing needs." The acting Librarian, William H. Bond, calls on "all our friends in the book world—dealers, collectors, scholars, and librarians" to help achieve this aim. Earlier in the year, Jackson had received an honorary degree, Litt.D., from Oxford and was elected to the Roxburghe Club.

Katharine F. Pantzer, Research Assistant to William A. Jackson, takes over the work of the *STC* after Jackson's death.

William H. Bond is named Lecturer in Bibliography at Harvard.

The Belknap Press publishes the first of a series of catalogues of the Printing and Graphic Arts collections, by Ruth Mortimer.

Acquisitions include a bull of Pope Paschal II dated October 28, 1113, possibly the oldest original papal bull in America; 375 volumes, chiefly editions of the classics and early Italian literature, from the library of the late Professor George Benson Weston, '97, presented by his son Charles D. Weston, '36; and 300 books from the library of the late Imrie de Vegh, Honorary Curator of Eastern European Literature and History, placed on deposit by Mrs. Richard T. Shields, the former Mrs. de Vegh.

Mabel A. E. Steele, Curator of the Keats Room, dies on December 11. Steele was also a Director and Chairman of the Editorial Board of the *Keats-Shelley Journal* from its founding in 1951, and the author of numerous articles on Keats.

By bequest Laura R. Evans establishes in memory of her son the William A. Evans, Jr. Fund for the Department of Printing and Graphic Arts. A gift from the Howard Bayne Fund is used to establish a fund in memory of Imrie de Vegh for the purchase of books, manuscripts and other relevant materials for the Department of Printing and Graphic Arts. The George Luther Lincoln, 1886 Bequest is established for the purchase of rare books and manuscripts and for other library purposes. The George Luther Lincoln, 1886 Publication Fund of the Harvard College Library is established for publications, the *Harvard Library Bulletin*, and acquisition of rare books and manuscripts.

EXHIBITIONS

Exhibition Room

Shakespeare, 1564–1964
Sixteenth-Century French Books
Sojourners in Far Worlds and Lost Lands
The World's Fair Revisited: The Great Exhibition in London 1851

Ground Floor

Ivan Fedorov

PUBLICATIONS

Delacroix's Faust: *Some Drawings and Lithographs for Goethe's* Faust *by Eugène Delacroix.* Cambridge, Department of Printing and Graphic Arts, Harvard College Library, 1964.
Ruth Mortimer, *French 16th-Century Books.* 2 volumes. Cambridge: Department of Printing and Graphic Arts, Harvard College Library, and the Belknap Press of Harvard University, 1964.

Wilmarth Sheldon Lewis and Philip Hofer, comp., *"The Beggar's Opera" by Hogarth and Blake: A Portfolio.* Cambridge: Harvard University Press; and New Haven and London: Yale University Press, 1964.

1965

William A. Jackson is awarded the gold medal of the Bibliographical Society of London, posthumously presented by Sir Frank Francis to Mrs. Jackson at Houghton. William H. Bond is appointed Librarian as of January 1.

Daniel Whitten becomes editor of the *Keats-Shelley Journal.*

Rodney G. Dennis becomes Curator of Manuscripts.

Roger E. Stoddard returns to the Houghton Library as Assistant Librarian after four years at Brown University. He is given responsibility for the acquisitions program.

James E. Walsh is named Keeper of Printed Books.

The Houghton Library is a major lender to the exhibition "2,000 Years of Calligraphy" organized by the Baltimore Museum of Art, the Peabody Institute Library, and the Walters Art Gallery, Baltimore.

The papers of Corinne Roosevelt Robinson are added to the Theodore Roosevelt Collection, the gift of her daughter, Corinne Robinson Alsop Cole.

Bayard L. Kilgour, Jr. is appointed Honorary Curator of the Slavic Collections in the College Library. Robert S. Pirie is appointed Honorary Curator of English Literature in the College Library,

Gifts from friends establish the William A. Jackson Fund, to facilitate the revival of the *Harvard Library Bulletin* as a living memorial.

EXHIBITIONS

Exhibition Room

Translation
T. S. Eliot: "In Memoriam"
Thomas Frognall Dibdin

PUBLICATIONS

William H. Bond, *The Houghton Library Report of Accessions for the Years 1963–65.* Cambridge, 1965.

The Gold Medal of the Bibliographical Society is posthumously presented to William A. Jackson, 1965.

William H. Bond.

William A. Jackson, *An Annotated List of the Publications of the Reverend Thomas Frognall Dibdin.* Edited by James E. Walsh and William H. Bond. Cambridge, 1966.

1966

The offices of the Theatre Collection collection move to Lamont Basement and a small reading room for eight people is established there. Access is through Lamont. At the same time, the Theatre Collection gets its first assistant curator, Arnold Wengrow.

The second volume of the Hours of Juana La Loca is placed on permanent deposit by Mrs. Adrian van Sinderen, joining the first volume, given to the Houghton Library in 1958 by three descendants of William White. The manuscript was divided into two volumes years ago and the two halves descended in different branches of the White family.

W. H. Bond begins teaching English 296, Descriptive and Analytical Bibliography, which will be offered every year from 1966 through 1985 and which will be continued by other staff members after that.

The Library continues to augment its collection of the papers and books of scientists and historians of science. Seven notebooks of George Sarton are added to letters and papers already at Harvard. Mrs. Percy W. Bridgman presents 29 volumes on theoretical physics and Mrs. Constance H. Hall gives the correspondence and personal papers of her father, Edwin Herbert Hall, including the manuscripts embodying his work on the electrical phenomenon known as the Hall effect.

Houghton participates in "Europe Informed: An Exhibition of Early Books which Acquainted Europe with the East." Other participating institutions include the New York Public Library, Columbia University Library, and the Library of the Hispanic Society of America.

In his annual report, Librarian William H. Bond identifies the most urgent problems facing Houghton as diminishing purchasing power in the face of rising prices and increasing demands and the lack of space for personnel and for the natural growth of the collections.

James E. Walsh makes his first book-buying trip to Europe as Keeper of Printed Books.

Eric H. L. Sexton is appointed Honorary Curator of Incunabula in the College Library. Leonard Baskin is appointed Honorary Curator of Typography and Illustration in the College Library. Fernando Zóbel is appointed Honorary Curator of Calligraphy in the College Library.

The Parkman D. Howe Fund is established for the purchase of rare books and manuscripts. Former students of George Parker Winship, 1893 establish in his memory the John Barnard Associates Fund to finance lectures at the Houghton Library.

EXHIBITIONS

Exhibition Room

A Selection of Books, Manuscripts, and Drawings Brought to the Department of Printing and Graphic Arts by Philip Hofer, '21 between 1938 and 1966

Fifty Novels in Manuscript

Luso-Brazilian Exhibition

PUBLICATIONS

Beatrix Potter: Letters to Children. Cambridge: Department
  of Printing and Graphic Arts, Harvard College Library;
  and New York: Walker & Co., 1966.
*A Selection of Books, Manuscripts, and Drawings Brought to
  the Department of Printing and Graphic Arts by Philip
  Hofer, '21, Between 1938 and 1966.* Cambridge: The
  Houghton Library, Harvard University, 1966.
Francis M. Rogers, *Europe Informed: An Exhibition of Early
  Books which Acquainted Europe with the East.* Cambridge
  and New York, 1966.
Rodney G. Dennis, "An Exhibition of Manuscripts in the
  Houghton Library," *Manuscripts,* 18 (1966), 40–42. Cat-
  alogue for "Fifty Novels in Manuscript."

1967

At a dinner on February 24 celebrating the
twenty-fifth anniversary of the Houghton Library, William H. Bond announces "birthday
presents" to the Library from its friends. In conjunction with the festivities, a special exhibition
of important items from Houghton collections
is installed in the second floor corridor.

The grant from the Ford Foundation (see
1957) being exhausted, the Bibliographical Society undertakes to raise funds for the research
on the *STC* not covered by the College Library.

William H. Bond is made Professor of Bibliography at Harvard.

At the commencement exercises on June 15,
Philip Hofer, Curator of Printing and Graphic
Arts, is awarded the degree of Doctor of Hu-
mane Letters.

William H. Bond at Houghton's 25th Birthday Party,
1967. Caricature by Fernando Zóbel.

EXHIBITIONS

Exhibition Room

Picasso
Writing Books
Vienna 1888–1938

PUBLICATIONS

William H. Bond, *The Houghton Library Reports XXIV and
  XXV, 1964–66.* Cambridge, 1967.
William A. Jackson, *Records of a Bibliographer: Selected
  Papers of William Alexander Jackson.* Ed. William H.
  Bond. Cambridge, 1967.
A Frog He Would A Wooing Go. From original designs by
  H. L. Stephens. Cambridge: Department of Printing and
  Graphic Arts, Harvard College Library; and New York:
  Walker and Co., 1967.
The Houghton Library 1942–1967. Compiled by William H.
  Bond; prefatory notes by Bond, James Walsh, and Phil-
  ip Hofer. Cambridge: Harvard College Library, 1967.

Philip Hofer, *Edward Lear as a Landscape Draughtsman.*
  Cambridge: The Belknap Press of Harvard University,
  1967.
Eugene M. Weber and James E. Walsh, *Vienna 1888–1938.*
  Cambridge: The Houghton Library, 1967. Exhibition
  catalogue.

1968

Philip Hofer retires as Curator of Printing and
Graphic Arts on June 30, 1968. He retains a
private office in the basement, adjoining a substantial stack area designated for his use. The
department he founded consolidates its position and presses on to new achievements under
the leadership of its new Curator, Peter A.

Wick, and its Associate Curator, Eleanor M. Garvey.

Jeanne T. Newlin joins the Theatre Collection as Assistant Curator on August 1.

Books and manuscripts from the Houghton Library are exhibited at Yale's Beinecke Library, and books and manuscripts from the Beinecke Library are exhibited at Houghton. Both institutions host visits by members of the Grolier Club. Prints and drawings by Honoré Daumier from the Houghton Library and from the collections of Philip Hofer and Arthur Vershbow are exhibited at the Fogg Art Museum.

Gifts from the Theodore Roosevelt Association enable the College Library to provide a curator for the Theodore Roosevelt Collection. Gregory C. Wilson is appointed to this position, under the jurisdiction of the Curator of Manuscripts, who presently chairs a College Library committee on the collection. The Association presents manuscripts of three books by Roosevelt and one thousand letters, and deposits papers of his sister, Anna Roosevelt Cowles.

The Codex Suprasliensis is offered to the Curator of Manuscripts for $20,000. This manuscript, the greatest monument to the history of Old Church Slavonic language, has been believed for decades to have perished during the fires in Warsaw at the end of World War II. After over a year of intrigue and subterfuge, a private donor is found to purchase the manuscript, which is then presented to the Polish government at a ceremony in Washington and returned to Warsaw where it belongs. This takes place in the middle of the Cold War.

Philip Hofer, '21 establishes the Philip and Frances Hofer Lecture Fund in the Department of Printing and Graphic Arts.

A. N. L. Munby delivers the first George Parker Winship Lecture on May 1. Leonard Baskin delivers the first Philip and Frances Hofer lecture on April 23.

Parkman D. Howe is appointed Honorary Curator of American Literature in the College Library.

EXHIBITIONS

Exhibition Room

Amy Lowell
Leonard Baskin

Edward Lear

Theatre Collection

Eugene O'Neill (Parts I and II)

LECTURES

Leonard Baskin, Honorary Curator of Typography and Illustration in the Harvard College Library, "The Graphic Arts: Three Aspects." The first Philip and Frances Hofer Lecture, in the Fogg Museum Lecture Hall. April 23, 1968.

A. N. L. Munby, "The Earl and the Thief: Lord Ashburnham and Count Libri." First George Parker Winship Lecture. May 1, 1968. Later published in the *Harvard Library Bulletin.*

Giovanni Mardersteig, "Leon Battista Alberti and the Revival of Roman Monumental Lettering in the Renaissance." Philip and Frances Hofer Lecture. December 5, 1968.

PUBLICATIONS

Eleanor M. Garvey, comp., *Philip Hofer as Author & Publisher.* Cambridge, 1968.

Juliet Kepes, *Birds.* Cambridge: Department of Printing and Graphic Arts, Harvard College Library; and New York: Walker & Co., 1968.

James Russell Lowell, *The Courtin'.* Illustrated by Winslow Homer. Facsimile of 1874 edition. Cambridge: Department of Printing and Graphic Arts, Harvard College Library; and New York: Walker & Co., 1968.

Edgar Allan Poe, *The Raven [Le Corbeau].* French translation by Stéphane Mallarmé. Illustrated by Édouard Manet. Facsimile of the edition of 1875. Introduction by Philip Hofer. Cambridge: Department of Printing and Graphic Arts, Harvard College Library; and New York: Walker & Co., 1968.

Two Poems by Emily Dickinson. Illustrated by Marie Angel. Cambridge: Department of Printing and Graphic Arts, Harvard College Library; and New York: Walker & Co., 1968.

Gustave Geffroy, *Yvette Guilbert.* Illustrated by Henri de Toulouse-Lautrec. English translation by Barbara Sessions. Introduction by Peter Wick. Cambridge: Department of Printing and Graphic Arts, Harvard College Library; and New York: Walker & Co., 1968.

1969

The Theatre Collection receives $1,000,000, given in memory of Robert Jordan by his widow, to provide space in the new underground addition to the College Library. The Theatre Collection is host to the International Theatre Research Congress, and stages special exhibitions on "The Player and the Playhouse" and on

"Harvard Men and Women of the Theatre" in honor of the occasion.

Volume V of the *BAL* (Washington Irving to Henry Wadsworth Longfellow) is published in March.

Beginning in June, the Harry Elkins Widener Collection, housed in the Widener Library building, is administered by the Houghton Library, with William H. Bond assuming, temporarily, the responsibilities of the Curator of the Widener Rooms.

On the night of Tuesday, August 19, during the hours when Widener Library is closed, an attempt is made to steal the Gutenberg Bible from the Widener Memorial Rooms. Entry is made by means of a rope from the roof of the Library building. During the attempt to regain the roof with the two large volumes in a knapsack, the intruder falls almost fifty feet to the interior concrete courtyard, sustaining serious injuries. He is apprehended when his moaning attracts the attention of a janitor.

Roger E. Stoddard becomes Associate Librarian of the Houghton Library

Philip Hofer receives the Donald F. Hyde Award from Princeton University.

Jeanne T. Newlin begins teaching Comp Lit 286 in the fall. A course by this title was previously offered by former Theatre Collection Curator William Van Lennep.

Thomas Edward Hanley, '15 establishes the Thomas Edward Hanley Bequest. The Billy Rose Foundation gives a fund, the income from which is to be used to create a Billy Rose Theatre Shelf in the Theatre Collection, with special emphasis on the American musical stage.

EXHIBITIONS

Exhibition Room

Erasmus: On the 500th Anniversary of his Birth

Theatre Collection

Boston Theatre: The Record of Will Rapport
The Player and the Playhouse
Harvard Men and Women of the Theatre

LECTURES

Boies Penrose, "English Printing at Antwerp in the Fifteenth Century." Second George Parker Winship Lecture. March 5, 1969. Later published in the *Harvard Library Bulletin*, v. 18.

Douglas H. Gordon, "The Book-collecting Northamptonshire Ishams and their Book-loving Virginia and Massachusetts Cousins." Third George Parker Winship Lecture. December 4, 1969. Later published in the *Harvard Library Bulletin*, v. 18.

PUBLICATIONS

William H. Bond, *The Houghton Library Reports XXVI and XXVII, 1966–68.* Cambridge, 1969.

Eleanor M. Garvey, *A'dilettanti delle bell'arti: A Decorated Alphabet Engraved by Giovanni Battista Betti, Florence, 1785.* Cambridge: Harvard College Library, Department of Printing and Graphic Arts, 1969.

Otto Benesch, *Artistic and Intellectual Trends from Rubens to Daumier As Shown in Book Illustration.* Cambridge: Department of Printing and Graphic Arts, Harvard College Library and New York, Walker & Co., 1969.

James E. Walsh, *Erasmus on the 500th Anniversary of His Birth.* Cambridge: The Houghton Library, 1969. Exhibition catalogue.

Othello: Fifteen Etchings by Théodore Chassériau. Introduction by Philip Hofer. Cambridge: Department of Printing and Graphic Arts, Harvard College Library; and New York, Walker & Co., 1969.

1970

During student demonstrations protesting the Vietnam War, Harvard Yard is locked every day at 5:00 p.m. Male staff members take turns spending the night in the Houghton Library, which is perceived as a possible target for demonstrators.

The opening of "The Turn of a Century," originally scheduled for May, is cancelled owing to demonstrations precipitated by the shootings at Kent State University. A "closing" is held instead of an opening, at the end of the exhibition run, in September.

Acquisitions include the *Cancionero de Oñate-Castañeda* (Spain, ca. 1480), an important and in some cases unique source for fifteenth-century Spanish poetry, the gift of Edwin M. Binney, 3rd; and Gioacchino Antonio Rossini, *Péchés de vieillesse*, containing many unpublished compositions, purchased with income from the Amy Lowell and Susan A. E. Morse Funds. P. James Roosevelt, '50 is appointed Honorary Curator of the Theodore Roosevelt Collection in the College Library.

Exhibition Room

Rara Astronomica

Documents in Early New England Church History (an exhibition held in connection with the annual meeting of the American Society of Church History)

The Turn of a Century, 1885–1910: Art Nouveau-Jugendstil Books

William King Richardson's Manuscripts

Ukrainian Incunabula, Manuscripts, Early Printed and Rare Books (partly from the collection of Bayard L. Kilgour, Jr., '27)

Widener Rotunda

John Ruskin

Sporting Books

The Author as Illustrator

LECTURES

Marcel Thomas, "The Library of Charles V of France and the Illuminations Ordered by Royal Command." Philip and Frances Hofer Lecture. March 19, 1970.

Hans A. Halbey, "Contemporary International Book Design and Illumination." Philip and Frances Hofer Lecture. October 13, 1970.

PUBLICATIONS

Leon Battista Alberti, *Ippolito e Lionora, from a Manuscript of Felice Feliciano in the Harvard College Library.* [Cambridge: Department of Printing and Graphic Arts, Harvard College Library], 1970.

Fernando Zóbel, *Cuenca: Sketchbook of a Spanish Hill Town.* Cambridge: Department of Printing and Graphic Arts, Harvard College Library; and New York: Walker & Co., 1970.

Eleanor Garvey, Anne B. Smith, and Peter A. Wick, *The Turn of a Century, 1885–1910: Art Nouveau-Jugendstil Books.* Cambridge: Department of Printing and Graphic Arts, The Houghton Library, Harvard University, 1970. Exhibition catalogue.

Philip Hofer, *Baroque Book Illustration, A Short Survey From the Collection in the Department of Printing and Graphic Arts, Harvard College Library.* 2nd edition. Cambridge: Harvard University Press, 1970.

Edward Kasinec, *Ukrainian Incunabula, Manuscripts, Early Printed and Rare Books.* Cambridge, 1970. Exhibition catalogue.

Owen Gingerich, *Rara Astronomica.* Cambridge, 1970. Exhibition catalogue, issued as a separate publication after its appearance in the *Harvard Library Bulletin.*

1971

The modern bust of John Keats is kidnapped from the Exhibition Room by undergraduates (and subsequently returned).

The Seventh International Congress of Bibliophiles meets in Boston, Philadelphia and New York. Registration is at the Houghton Library on the afternoon of September 29. Special exhibitions, including many unique items which the Congress could not see elsewhere, are mounted in its honor in the Exhibition Room, the Theatre Collection, the Printing and Graphic Arts Study Room, and the Keats, Lowell and Richardson Rooms. A small exhibit in the Chaucer Case is devoted to the work of William A. Jackson and the continuation of his revision of the *STC*.

Wallace F. Dailey of the Widener Catalog Department is appointed Curator of the Theodore Roosevelt Collection, replacing Gregory C. Wilson.

EXHIBITIONS

Exhibition Room

John Keats

Scientific Books and Instruments from the Collection of David P. Wheatland, '22

Exhibition Honoring the Seventh International Congress of Bibliophiles

English Eighteenth-Century Bindings

Dürer and German Book Illustration of the Renaissance

Sixteenth-Century Architectural Books from Italy and France

Printing and Graphic Arts Room

Reynolds Stone

PUBLICATIONS

Marie Angel, *An Animated Alphabet.* Cambridge: Department of Printing and Graphic Arts, Harvard College Library, 1971.

Peter A. Wick, *Sixteenth-Century Architectural Books from Italy and France.* Cambridge: Department of Printing and Graphic Arts, Harvard College Library, 1971. Exhibition catalogue.

Boswell, Johnson, and the Petition of James Wilson. Cambridge, The Houghton Library, 1971. A facsimile reproduction of one of Boswell's Court of Session legal papers, the most important part of which was written by Samuel Johnson. Preface by William H. Bond. Published as a keepsake for a meeting of the Johnsonians.

William H. Bond, *The Houghton Library.* Cambridge, 1971. A brief pamphlet of necessary information for readers, the first such to be published by the Houghton Library.

Sidney E. Ives, *VII International Congress of Bibliophiles, Boston Program.* Cambridge, 1971. Includes the illustrated catalogue of the exhibition.

THE FOURTH DECADE: 1972–1981

Pusey Library under construction, ca. 1973.

Manuscript stacks in Pusey basement.

1972

Helen Willard retires on June 30 as Curator of the Theatre Collection, a position she has held for twelve years. Jeanne T. Newlin is the new Curator.

An exhibition of "Books and Book Covers by Toulouse-Lautrec" is part of a six-institution Toulouse-Lautrec festival, involving the Fogg Art Museum, M.I.T., Boston University, the Boston Public Library, and the Museum of Fine Arts, as well as the Houghton Library.

M–S, T–V and I–K of the *STC* are sent to the printer. L should be next, but proves worse than expected, due to difficult headings, especially "Lily's Grammar," "Liturgies," and "London."

Earle E. Coleman is granted leave from Princeton University Archives (through June 1974) to work on completing the *BAL*.

The gift of Mrs. John W. Valentine is used to establish the John Wadsworth Valentine, '29 Book Fund for the purchase of books and manuscripts, with the preference being given to English literature and history.

EXHIBITIONS

Exhibition Room

Beerbohm, Beardsley, Rothenstein: A Centennial View
Books and Book Covers by Toulouse-Lautrec
Early Botanical Books: An Exhibit Celebrating the Centennial of the Arnold Arboretum, 1872–1972
The Great Campaigns of Theodore Roosevelt

Theatre Collection

Twentieth-Century Stage Design

Widener Rotunda

Ezra Pound

LECTURES

Anthony Hobson, "The Quest for Canevari." Philip and Frances Hofer Lecture. April 25, 1972.
Jakob Rosenberg, "Toulouse-Lautrec and his Favorite Models." Philip and Frances Hofer Lecture. December 13, 1972.
Philip Hofer, "Calligraphy and Manuscripts in the Eastern World." Fourth George Parker Winship Lecture. October 25, 1972.

PUBLICATIONS

Eleanor M. Garvey, *The Artist and the Book, 1860–1960 in Western Europe and the United States.* 2nd edition. Cambridge: Department of Printing and Graphic Arts, Harvard College Library; and Boston: The Museum of Fine Arts, 1972.
Jan van Krimpen, *A Letter to Philip Hofer on Certain Problems Connected with the Mechanical Cutting of Punches.* A facsimile reproduction and commentary by John Dreyfus. No. 4 in the Studies in the History of Calligraphy. Cambridge: Department of Printing and Graphic Arts, Harvard College Library; and Boston: David R. Godine, 1972.
Early Botanical Books: An Exhibit Celebrating the Centennial of the Arnold Arboretum 1872–1972. Cambridge, The Houghton Library [1972]. Exhibition catalogue.
Toulouse-Lautrec Book Covers and Brochures. Preface by Peter A. Wick. Department of Printing and Graphic Arts, Harvard College Library, 1972.
Helen D. Willard, *Twentieth-Century Stage Design.* Cambridge, 1972. Exhibition checklist.
Judaica in the Houghton Library. Cambridge, 1972. Reduced offset reproductions in book form from Houghton Library catalogue cards.

1973

Final plans submitted by Hugh Stubbins and Associates for the new Pusey Library are approved in March. The Theatre Collection is to be housed in a portion of the new building. The second level will include stack areas for the Houghton Manuscript Collection.

W–Z of the *STC* is sent to the printer in May.

For two years beginning in June, the ground surrounding the Houghton Library is completely taken up with the building of the Pusey Library, and it is impossible to hold exhibitions and lectures in Houghton. Uninterrupted access for readers and staff is maintained during this period through the Widener stack and the bridge.

Volume VI of the *BAL* (Augustus Baldwin Longstreet to Thomas William Parsons) is published in December.

Roger E. Stoddard makes his first book-buying trip to London and Paris. Thereafter he alternates with James E. Walsh, who covers Scandinavia, the Netherlands, Germany, and Austria.

Major acquisitions include a collection of German plays, mainly printed in Vienna between 1730 and 1790, purchased with the George L. Lincoln Fund; papers of Joseph Severn, an addition to Severn papers already in the

Harvard Keats Collection, the gift of Arthur A. Houghton, Jr.; and the autograph album of Count Sergei Yulevich Witte (1849–1915), containing 176 letters, documents and manuscripts of the eighteenth and nineteenth centuries, the gift of Bayard L. Kilgour, Jr. Fifty-three engravings of the *"Presentazione della Chinea"* (1724–1785) plus nine descriptive pamphlets (1663–1767) are presented to the Department of Printing and Graphic Arts by Franklin H. Kissner.

David P. Wheatland is appointed Honorary Curator of the Collection of Historical Scientific Instruments.

The John Gilman D'Arcy Paul, '08 Bequest is established for the Houghton Library. The Joseph Halle Schaffner Book Fund is established for the purchase of rare books and manuscripts. The gift of Augustus P. Loring is used to establish the Brybo Book Fund in honor of Douglas Bryant and William H. Bond.

Exhibition Room

Rudolph Ruzicka: An Exhibition of Illustration, Design and Typography
The 500th Anniversary of Copernicus

Printing and Graphic Arts Room

Rowlandson

Ruth Mortimer, "A Portrait of the Author in Sixteenth-Century Italy." Philip and Frances Hofer Lecture. March 20, 1973.

Walter Oakeshott, "Some English Painters of the late Twelfth Century." Fifth George Parker Winship Lecture. January 23, 1973.
Graham Pollard, "Jacob Golius and Books from the East." Sixth George Parker Winship Lecture. Held in the Lamont Library Forum Room owing to the construction of Pusey. December 13, 1973.

Rosamond B. Loring, *Decorated Book Papers, Being an Account of Their Designs and Fashions,* 3rd edition. Cambridge, Department of Printing and Graphic Arts, Harvard College Library, 1973.
Department of Printing and Graphic Arts, *Publications in Print 1973.* (A leaflet listing 23 books and pamphlets, 25 color reproductions, 14 Christmas cards, 9 color postcards, 15 black and white postcards, and 21 correspondence folders with envelopes.)

1974

Major acquisitions include literary manuscripts and correspondence of Robert Lowell and forty books from the library of Frédéric Lachèvre, both purchased with the Amy Lowell Fund; a fine-paper copy of Frank Lloyd Wright's *Ausgeführte Bauten und Entwürfe* (Berlin, 1940), given by Philip Hofer in honor of Fernando Zóbel, '49; and 101 drawings by Jean Hugo for Carl Dreyer's film, *La passion de Jeanne d'Arc* (1928), purchased with the Francis Cabot Lowell, Robert Gould Shaw and Edward Sheldon Funds.

William H. Bond becomes President of the

Librarians visiting Pusey construction site: Jeanne T. Newlin, Robert Walsh, Harley P. Holden, Rita Paddock, Clark Elliott, Charles Montalbano, and Roger E. Stoddard, ca. 1973.

Bibliographical Society of America.

On the *STC,* the revision of L is finally completed and sent to the printer (see 1972).

An exhibition of drawings by the architect H. H. Richardson, organized by James F. O'Gorman and the Department of Printing and Graphic Arts, is shown at the Fogg Art Museum, the Albany Institute of History and Art and the Renwick Gallery in Washington, D.C.

The Belknap Press publishes the second of Ruth Mortimer's catalogues of the Printing and Graphic Arts collections.

Jacob Blanck, editor of the *BAL,* dies on December 23. He is succeeded by his last assistant, Katherine S. Jarvis.

William Bentinck-Smith, '37 and other friends establish the Jacob Blanck Fund for books and manuscripts of scholarly importance, with preference for materials of the period embraced by the *Bibliography of American Literature* of which Blanck was so long the editor.

EXHIBITIONS

Exhibition Room

Poetics and Music

Amy Lowell Room

Ukrainian Imprints

Theatre Collection

The Player-King: Shakespeare's Histories on the Stage

Widener Lobby

Exhibition in honor of Arthur Colby Sprague, '19 (mounted by the Theatre Collection)

Widener Rotunda

Reflections in the Middle East
Hugo von Hofmannsthal, 1874–1929
Thomas Hollis

PUBLICATIONS

William H. Bond, *The Houghton Library Reports XXVIII and XXIX, 1968–70.* Cambridge, 1974.

James F. O'Gorman, *H. H. Richardson and his Office, Selected Drawings. A Centennial of his Move to Boston 1874.* Preface by Peter A. Wick. [Cambridge]: Department of Printing and Graphic Arts, Harvard College Library, 1974. Exhibition catalogue.

Ruth Mortimer, *Italian 16th-Century Books.* 2 Volumes. Cambridge: Department of Printing and Graphic Arts, Harvard College Library and Belknap Press, 1974.

James E. Walsh, *The Hofmannsthal Collection in the Houghton Library.* Heidelberg: Lothar Stiehm Verlag, 1974.

Three Portrait Drawings by Henri Matisse with a Letter by Matthew S. Prichard describing their Creation in Paris, 1913. With notes by Philip Hofer, Walter Muir Whitehill, and Samuel D. Warren. Cambridge: Department of Printing and Graphic Arts, Harvard College Library, 1974.

The Player-King: Shakespeare's Histories on the Stage. Cambridge, 1974. Preface by Jeanne T. Newlin. Exhibition checklist.

1975

Eleanor M. Garvey becomes Curator of Printing and Graphic Arts, succeeding Peter A. Wick.

Roger E. Stoddard succeeds William H. Bond as Chairman of the Bibliographical Society of America Supervisory Committee for the *BAL.* He hires Virginia L. Smyers as editor, a position she will hold until 1982, and submits a grant application to the NEH.

Katharine F. Pantzer, Bibliographer in the Houghton Library, receives a grant from the National Endowment for the Humanities for work on the revision of the *STC.* This is the first of five grants from NEH in support of this project. Matching funds are provided at different times by the Leverhulme Foundation and the Andrew W. Mellon Foundation. A second grant from the National Endowment for the Humanities provides funding for processing and filming the archives of the Republic of Georgia. The work is carried out by Prince Nakašidze of Georgia.

Major acquisitions include Johannes Regiomontanus, *Calendario* (Venice, 1476), the earliest book to have a title-page with an imprint, and other incunabula, the gift of Philip Hofer; five sixteenth-century publishers' catalogues, four of them previously unrecorded, the gift of the Friends of the Harvard College Library; a collection of 608 eighteenth- and nineteenth-century chapbooks from the library of Henry Huth, purchased with the Amy Lowell Fund; and Blaise Cendrars, *La Prose du Transsibérien* (Paris, 1913), one of 60 copies with stencilled designs by Sonia Delaunay, the gift of the Friends of the Harvard College Library.

Peter A. Wick is appointed Honorary Curator of Architectural Books in the College Library.

Francis W. Hatch, '19 establishes the Francis W. Hatch Book Fund in the Harvard Theatre Collection; it is later augmented by family and friends. The John Cutter, '09 Bequest is established by residuary bequest, the income to be divided between the Fogg Art Museum and the Houghton Library.

EXHIBITIONS

Exhibition Room

The Centenary of Rainer Maria Rilke (largely from the
  collection of Richard von Mises)
Eric Gill

Widener Rotunda

Audubon Drawings
Bicentennial Show

LECTURES

John Dreyfus, "Eric Gill as Type Designer and Book Illustrator." October 30, 1975.

PUBLICATIONS

Department of Printing and Graphic Arts, *Publications in Print 1975.*

Mordechai Glatzer, *Hebrew Manuscripts in the Houghton Library.* Edited by Charles Berlin and Rodney Dennis. Cambridge, 1975.
Die Weise von Leibe und Tod des Cornets Otto Rilke (geschrieben 1899) [von] Rainer Maria Rilke. Cambridge, 1975. Facsimile keepsake.

1976

The Nathan Marsh Pusey Library is dedicated on May 1. The Theatre Collection moves into its new quarters, which include a reading room, exhibition rooms, offices and stack space.

The Theodore Roosevelt Reading Alcove in the Widener Library and the Theodore Roosevelt Gallery in the new Pusey Library are dedicated on Wednesday afternoon, June 9. The latter is a gift of the Theodore Roosevelt Association and family members. Rare books, pictures, and scrapbooks from the Widener portion of the Theodore Roosevelt Collection are moved to Houghton and shelved with the Roosevelt manuscripts in the Houghton stacks in Pusey.

James E. Walsh and Mollie Della Terza presenting a Kitchenaid mixer to John Lancaster and Ruth Mortimer, 1975.

The re-opening of Houghton's front door is celebrated with a party. The Houghton staff gathers in the lobby to drink champagne, while the door, which has been closed during construction of Pusey, is opened to a recording of the "Prisoners' Hymn to the Light" from the second act of *Fidelio.*

Carolyn Jakeman retires after thirty-four years in charge of the Houghton Reading Room. Marte Shaw succeeds her.

Scolar Press publishes a facsimile of Henry James's *The American: The Version of 1877;* the original is in Houghton.

Michael Winship joins *BAL* as a research assistant.

Volume II (the first volume to be published) of the *STC* is published in May.

Major acquisitions include five works by Albrecht Dürer, the gift of Philip Hofer; Russian books from the Diaghilev-Lifar sale, the gift of Bayard L. Kilgour, Jr.; the third known copy of John Baskerville's type specimen of ca. 1762, the gift of William Bentinck-Smith; and manuscript poems and papers of Pedro Salinas, including 1079 letters to his wife, ca. 1914–51, the gift of Mrs. Juan Marichal and Mr. Jaime Salinas.

Edwin Binney, 3rd is appointed Honorary Curator of Ballet in the Harvard Theatre Collection. Carolyn E. Jakeman is appointed Honorary Curator of American Missionary Papers in the Harvard College Library.

A grant from the George H. Mifflin and Jane A. Mifflin Memorial Fund by their son George Harrison Mifflin, 1900 is used to establish a fund for the purchase of rare books and manuscripts. The Charlotte and Arthur Vershbow Book Fund for the purchase of books for the Department of Printing and Graphic Arts is established.

EXHIBITIONS

Exhibition Room

Accessions to the Collection of Ukrainian Rare Books and Manuscripts, 1973–76

Lawyer, Doctor, Farmer, Merchant, Clergyman, Statesman: Signers of the Declaration of Independence

Fact and Fantasy, Illustrated Books from a Private Collection

Australiana in the Harvard Libraries

Plaster ceiling panel for the Hyde Rooms, 1977.

A Selection of Association and Presentation Copies Collected by Amy Lowell

Widener Rotunda

Edward Gibbon

Theodore Roosevelt Gallery

The Many Faces of Theodore Roosevelt

LECTURES

Bernard M. Rosenthal, "Cartel, Clan, or Dynasty? The Olschkis and the Rosenthals, 1859–1976." Seventh George Parker Winship Lecture. April 18, 1976. (Later published in the *Harvard Library Bulletin.*)

John Lowe, "Early Views of Japan." November 6, 1976.

Lloyd J. Reynolds, "From Script to Print and the Revival of Script." December 2, 1976.

PUBLICATIONS

David P. Becker, *Fact and Fantasy. Illustrated Books from a Private Collection.* Cambridge: Department of Printing and Graphic Arts, Harvard College Library, 1976. Exhibition catalogue.

James E. Walsh (ed.), *1848 Austrian Revolutionary Broadsides and Pamphlets, A Catalogue.* Boston: G. K. Hall & Co., 1976.

James E. Walsh (ed.), *Mazarinades, A Catalogue.* Boston: G. K. Hall, 1976.

Kenneth E. Carpenter, *Russian Revolutionary Literature Collection, Houghton Library.* New Haven: Research Publications, 1976.

1977

On September 16, 1977, Dr. Johnson's birthday, the Johnsonians hold their annual dinner at 17 Quincy Street, followed by a preview of the Donald Hyde Rooms on the second floor of the

Houghton Library. The Donald Hyde Rooms, created to honor the late Donald Hyde by his widow, Mary Hyde, and his friend, Arthur A. Houghton, Jr., open to the public the next day, following more than ten years of planning, remodeling and furnishing. Designed by Conover Fitch, Jr., of Perry, Dean, and Stewart, successors to the firm that designed the Houghton Library, the Rooms include an entry hall, oval exhibition room, reading room, secretarial office, curator's office, scholar's room and stacks. The plaster ceiling and the capitals in the exhibition room and the decorations in the entry hall are based on drawings by Robert Adam in Sir John Soane's Museum, London, and were made from original Adam molds.

A profile of Katharine F. Pantzer appears in the *New Yorker*.

[Mrs. Mary Hyde], *The Donald Hyde Rooms in the Houghton Library, Harvard University*. Cambridge, 1977. Pamphlet issued for the opening of the Hyde Rooms.

1978

The Library is closed during the Blizzard of 1978. During the days that follow, staff members who live nearby keep the Reading Room open although roads remain impassable throughout much of the state.

A grant from the National Endowment for the Humanities enables the Houghton Library to microfilm its manuscript accessions records and indexes, covering acquisitions of the Library since it opened in 1942, and giving dates of acquisition, sources, funds and prices, as well as inventories of manuscript collections. This is done so that Houghton holdings will be fully

View of the Hyde Rooms. *Photo by Diane Asséo Griliches.*

Keyes D. Metcalf, Katharine F. Pantzer, Rene Bryant, and Mrs. Donald Hyde at the opening of the Hyde Rooms, 1977.

reported in the National Union Catalogue of Manuscript Collections.

The National Endowment for the Humanities also takes over the major burden of funding the *BAL*. The Lilly Endowment continues to provide supplemental funding.

The Frances L. Hofer Bequest of over 1500 drawings for book illustration, including works by Rubens, Delacroix and Picasso, comes to the Department of Printing and Graphic Arts.

Through a residuary bequest of Josephine Waters Bennett the Roger Enoch and Josephine Waters Bennett Fund is established for the repair of books printed before 1700.

EXHIBITIONS

Exhibition Room

Jean-Jacques Rousseau
A Selection of Manuscripts Relating to the Art of Poetry, purchased from 1975 to 1977 with funds presented by the

Witter Bynner Foundation
Lewis Carroll Exhibition
William Blake, 1757–1827 (joint exhibition with Fogg Art Museum)
Shelley and his Circle: Additions to the Carl H. Pforzheimer Library 1957–1978: for the Fiftieth Reunion of Harvard '28

Keats Room

B. R. Haydon

Amy Lowell Room

Eighteenth-Century English Literary Manuscripts

Ground Floor

Wendell Phillips

Theatre Collection

Gilbert and Sullivan Miscellany: A Century of the Operas on Stage
John Lindquist, Photographer: 40 Years of American Dance
Class Reunion Exhibition: Harvard on Stage
Renaissance Theatre in Northern Italy: The Court and the City
History of Hasty Pudding Theatricals (in Widener)

Theodore Roosevelt Gallery

Father and Daughter: Theodore Roosevelt and Ethel Carow Roosevelt Derby

LECTURES

Mirjam M. Foot, "A Talk on Bookbinding." Eighth George Parker Winship Lecture. February 2, 1978.

Andrew Wilton, "Blake as a Landscape Artist." Philip and Frances Hofer Lecture. February 24, 1978.

Adrian Wilson, "The Making of the Nuremberg Chronicle." Philip and Frances Hofer Lecture. April 5, 1978.

Douglas H. Gordon, Ninth George Parker Winship Lecture. May 18, 1978.

John Dreyfus, "The Calligraphy and Type Designs of Edward Johnston." Philip and Frances Hofer Lecture. November 1, 1978.

PUBLICATIONS

Tenniel's Alice: Drawings by Sir John Tenniel for Alice's Adventures in Wonderland and Through the Looking Glass. Introduction by Eleanor M. Garvey and W. H. Bond. Cambridge: Department of Printing and Graphic Arts, Harvard College Library; and New York: The Metropolitan Museum of Art, 1978.

Eleanor M. Garvey, comp., *Philip Hofer as Author & Publisher: A Supplement.* Cambridge: Department of Printing and Graphic Arts, 1978.

Shelley and his Circle: Additions to the Carl H. Pforzheimer Library 1957–1978. [Cambridge:] The Houghton Library, 1978.

1979

Research Publications, Inc., of Woodbridge, Connecticut begins work on a project for publication in microfilm of playbills from the Harvard Theatre Collection, including primarily nineteenth-century material from some fifteen London theatres.

The Scholars Press of Missoula publishes a list of Syriac manuscripts in Houghton, by Moshe H. Goshen-Gottstein.

Former Theatre Collection curator Helen Willard dies on May 5.

Acquisitions include manuscripts by L. E. Sissman.

Mrs. Henry Ware Eliot is appointed Honorary Curator of the Eliot Collection in the Houghton Library.

EXHIBITIONS

Exhibition Room

Decorated Papers: A Selection from the Loring Collection

Gothic Fantasy in English and American Literature

Gifts of Arthur A. Houghton, Jr.: Fiftieth Reunion Exhibition

The Amy Lowell Bequest: Houghton Library Books and Manuscripts Acquired in the First Twenty-five Years

Manuscripts and First Editions of Classical Authors (for the American Philological Association and the Archæological Institute of America)

Ground Floor

Selections from E. E. Cummings Manuscripts

Theatre Collection

History of the Out-of-Doors: An American Dramatic Tradition

Commencement Exhibition: History of Theatre at Radcliffe in honor of the Radcliffe Centenary

Class Reunion Exhibition: Harvard on Stage

Publishing for Dance: William Como *Dance Magazine* Collection

The Theatre of Samuel Beckett in the Seventies

Widener Lobby

Winner of Five Academy Awards: John Green, '28 (mounted by the Theatre Collection)

Widener Rotunda

Drawings by John Ruskin

James Cook: An Eighteenth-Century Scientist

Theodore Roosevelt Gallery

The Presidential Campaigns of 1904, 1908, and 1912

LECTURES

Anthony Hobson, "English Library Interiors from Thomas Bodley to Horace Walpole." Tenth George Parker Winship Lecture. February 26, 1979.

James Mosley, "The Caslons and Eighteenth-Century English Type-founding." Philip and Frances Hofer Lecture. April 12, 1979.

Dorothy Abbe, "The Art of William Addison Dwiggins." Philip and Frances Hofer Lecture. November 7, 1979.

PUBLICATIONS

Sidney E. Ives, *The Houghton Library Reports XXX–XXXIV, 1970–75.* Cambridge, 1979. Foreword and afterword by William H. Bond.

Keepsake for the Harvard Class of 1929: Facsimile of Jonathan Swift, *A Modest Proposal* (1729). Cambridge, 1979.

1980

Amid extensive press and television coverage, some 17,500 letters written by Leon Trotsky during his exile are opened to the public on January 2, 1980. These form approximately one-third of the papers that were acquired in the 1940s from Trotsky and his widow with the stipulation that the "Exile Papers" remain closed until 1980 to protect Trotsky's associates. Acquisition of the Trotsky papers was made possible by the generosity of John W. Blodgett, Jr., '23 and his daughter, Mrs. Katherine Winter, '63. On the same day, F. Thomas Noonan assumes his duties as Curator of the Reading Room.

Hugh Amory receives a Munby Fellowship at Cambridge University Library.

The unveiling of the model of Shakespeare's Globe Playhouse, the gift of Stanley J. Kahrl, is celebrated in the Theatre Collection during a meeting of the Shakespeare Association of America.

Grants from the Kress Foundation and the National Endowment for the Humanities provide for the microfilming of manuscripts written before 1600 and for the color and black and white photography of 3,000 miniatures and important initials. This is done for the purpose of preservation, because the manuscripts are being so heavily used that it is feared they will deteriorate.

Philip Hofer, D.F.A.

The Harvard-Radcliffe Manuscripts and Archives Group is founded, Rodney G. Dennis serving on the steering committee.

William H. Bond and Katy Homans teach a course in the history and practice of letterpress printing, with studio sessions at The Bow and Arrow Press in Adams House.

The Houghton Library Fund is established to support staff positions. Philip Hofer, '21 establishes the Printing and Graphic Arts Acquisition Fund.

EXHIBITIONS

Exhibition Room

Trotsky, on the Occasion of the Opening of the Exile Papers
Medieval and Renaissance Manuscripts, Illuminations, and Book Hands, 750–1600
Drawings for Book Illustration
Roman Books from the Collection of Franklin H. Kissner
Materials for the Study of Publishing History
Spanish Literature in the Golden Age
A Selection of French Literary Manuscripts, 1600–1960
Russian Books of the Avant-Garde
Quevedo and his Age, 1580–1980
Montaigne's *Essais*, 1580–1980
The Library of Jacques-August de Thou
The Ostrih Bible, 1580/81–1980/81

Theatre Collection

Restoration and Eighteenth-Century Theatre
Shakespeare's First Globe Playhouse
Bournonville Dancing

Theodore Roosevelt Gallery

Theodore Roosevelt at Harvard
Theodore Roosevelt, 1900–1901: Governor, Vice-President, President.

LECTURES

Jean van Heijenoort, "The History of Trotsky's Papers." January 7, 1980. Published in the *Harvard Library Bulletin*, 28 (1980).
Barbara Tuchman, David McCullough, and Edmund Morris. Talks on the centennial of Theodore Roosevelt's graduation from Harvard College. May 9, 1980.
Hans Schmoller, "The Microcosm of Decorated Paper." Philip and Frances Hofer Lecture. October 21, 1980.
Ian Willison, "The British Museum Library: Early Benefactors from Sloan to Grenville." Eleventh George Parker Winship Lecture. October 27, 1980.
John E. Bowlt, "A Slap in the Face of Public Taste: Book Design and the Russian Avant-Garde." Philip and Frances Hofer Lecture. December 2, 1980.

PUBLICATIONS

Sidney E. Ives, *The Houghton Library Reports XXXV–XXXVI, 1975–77*. Cambridge, 1980. Foreword and afterword by William H. Bond. This was the last such report to be published.

Roger E. Stoddard, *Ten Roman Etchings by Melchior Küsel (1622–1683): From the Collection of Franklin H. Kissner*. Cambridge: The Houghton Library, 1980. Exhibition keepsake.

David P. Becker, *Drawings for Book Illustration. The Hofer Collection*. Cambridge: Department of Printing and Graphic Arts, The Houghton Library, 1980. Exhibition catalogue.

David Wood, *Music in the Harvard Libraries. A Catalogue of Early Printed Music and Books on Music in the Houghton Library and the Eda Kuhn Loeb Music Library*. Cambridge: Harvard University Press, 1980.

The Ostrih Bible 1580/81–1980/81. A Quadricentennial Exhibition. Cambridge: The Houghton Library, Harvard University, 1980.

Index Librorum Prohibitorum (1559), ed. Roger E. Stoddard. Cambridge, 1980. Facsimile published for members of the Rare Books and Manuscripts Section of A.C.R.L.

Stanley J. Kahrl, C. Walter Hodges, David Bevington and Jeanne T. Newlin, *Shakespeare's First Globe Theatre: The Harvard Theatre Collection Model Designed by C. Walter Hodges*. Cambridge, Harvard Theatre Collection, Harvard College Library, 1980.

1981

The Theatre Collection celebrates its eightieth anniversary in November with a reception and exhibition, followed by a dinner for benefactors and friends of the collection.

Harvard University Press publishes a facsimile of the Emily Dickinson manuscripts in Houghton, edited by Ralph W. Franklin to restore the state and order in which the poet left them.

The series "Chamber Music in the Houghton Library" is inaugurated in an effort to draw the public into the Library and to increase Harvard's role in presenting chamber music to the greater Boston community. Musicians and programs are selected by a committee consisting of Louis Krasner, Christoph Wolff, and Rodney G. Dennis (Secretary).

The Thomas Wolfe Association of America holds its annual meeting at the Houghton Library; the proceedings appear in 1982 as *Thomas Wolfe: A Harvard Perspective*.

Dr. Henry A. Murray, '15 establishes the Henry A. Murray Fund for the Papers of American Literary Authors in the Houghton Library for acquisition, processing, and reference. Howard Phipps, Jr., '55 establishes the Howard Phipps, Jr. Endowment Fund for cataloguing printed books. Frederick R. Koch and other friends establish the Theatre Collection 80th Anniversary Fund. Mr. and Mrs. Theodore

Rodney G. Dennis and Suzanne Currier, ca. 1980.

Roger E. Stoddard, Anne Anninger, and Katharine F. Pantzer (in background).

Sherwood Hope, Jr. establish a book fund for the Department of Printing and Graphic Arts, to be used to purchase books on printing and the art of the book, including the life and works of William Morris. The Viscountess Eccles establishes a trust ultimately to endow the Donald and Mary Hyde Fund for the acquisition of rare books and manuscripts for the Houghton Library.

EXHIBITIONS

Exhibition Room

Arno Werner, Master Bookbinder

German Illustrated Books from the Sixteenth Century: The Gift of Philip Hofer, '21

Selections from the Harcourt Amory Collection of Lewis Carroll

Presentazione della Chinea

Eighteenth-Century Science: An Exhibit of Books and Manuscripts from Harvard Collections

Andrea Palladio and his Influence: Three Centuries of Illustrated Books

Somos Poetas! Poetas! Garcia Lorca, Guillén, Salinas

Ground Floor

Peiresc

Theatre Collection

Theatre Art of the Medici

The Past is Prologue: Treasures of the Harvard Theatre Collection

Widener Rotunda

Lucretius, *De Rerum Natura:* A Printing History

Theodore Roosevelt Gallery

A Cartoon Biography of Theodore Roosevelt

Ticknor Lounge

Fiftieth Anniversary of the Death of Lauro de Bosis

LECTURES

Alois M. Nagler, "*Commedia dell'arte* at the Bavarian Court." Twelfth George Parker Winship Lecture. January 16, 1981.

Stephen Harvard, "Cataneo and the Living Alphabet." Philip and Frances Hofer Lecture. October 27, 1981.

Hugh Amory, Martha Mahard, Rodney G. Dennis and Jeanne T. Newlin at "Bonefeast," 1981.

Lotte Hellinga, "Patron and Printer: Margaret of York and Caxton." Thirteenth George Parker Winship Lecture. November 23, 1981.

Terisio Pignatti, "Venetian Architecture: The View Painters' Approach." Philip and Frances Hofer Lecture. December 8, 1981.

CONCERTS

Harvey Seigal, violin; Michael Zaretsky, viola; Martha Babcock, cello. Schubert, Beethoven, and Mozart. October 23, 1981.

Masuko Ushioda, violin; Laurence Lesser, cello. Beethoven, Bach, and Ravel. November 10, 1981.

PUBLICATIONS

James F. Walsh, *Arno Werner, Master Bookbinder.* Cambridge: The Houghton Library, 1981. Exhibition catalogue.

Arno Werner, *Arno Werner on Bookbinding.* Cambridge: The Houghton Library, 1981.

Colin Cohen, *The James McBey Collection of Watermarked Paper.* Introduction by Nicolas Barker. Cambridge: The Houghton Library, 1981.

The Bute Broadsides in the Houghton Library. Introd. by Hugh Amory. Woodbridge, Connecticut: Research Publications, Inc., 1981.

Stephen Harvard, *An Italic Copybook: The Cataneo Manuscript.* [Cambridge]: Department of Printing and Graphic Arts, The Houghton Library, 1981.

Suzanne N. H. Currier, "An Exhibition of French Literary Manuscripts, 1600–1960," *Harvard Library Bulletin,* 29 (1981), 217–224. Checklist of the 1980 exhibition.

Harvard Theatre Collection. *The Theatre: 1982 Engagement Book.* New York: Abbeville Press, 1981.

Ars Memorandi: *A Facsimile of the Text and Woodcuts Printed by Thomas Anshelm at Pforzheim in 1502.* [Cambridge]: Department of Printing and Graphic Arts, The Houghton Library, 1981.

Roger S. Wieck, "An Exhibition of German Illustrated Books from the Sixteenth Century: The Gift of Philip Hofer," *Harvard Library Bulletin,* 29 (1981), 332–336. Exhibition checklist.

THE FIFTH DECADE: 1982–1991

Manuel M. Sadagursky in the Houghton Lobby.

James Lewis in the Reading Room. *Photo by Diane Asséo Griliches.*

1982

The Houghton Library celebrates its fortieth anniversary with a weekend of festivities culminating on February 27 with a formal opening of an exhibition of books and manuscripts acquired by the Library during the past fifteen years. Major gifts to the fund for the support of the Houghton Library are announced at a Friday night dinner for friends and benefactors. A book-shaped birthday cake is cut by William H. Bond using a replica of Excalibur by Steuben Glass. Other events of the weekend include workshops and tours of the Library conducted by staff members. On March 6, former and current staff gather to share memories, photographs, and a day of special events, including a performance by Harvard's Gilbert and Sullivan Players in honor of Mr. and Mrs. Bond. Subsequently, the exhibition is expanded by 100 additional items and shown at the Grolier Club in New York from December 21, 1982 through February 5, 1983. Special events there include a reception for Library benefactors and Grolier Club members and a lecture by Roger Stoddard.

At the end of June, William H. Bond retires as Librarian of the Houghton Library, a position he has occupied since the death of William A. Jackson in 1964. His responsibilities are assumed by Lawrence Dowler, Associate Librarian of Harvard College. Bond is appointed Sandars Reader in Bibliography, Cambridge University, and delivers four public lectures there on Thomas Hollis of Lincoln's Inn.

Houghton begins machine accessioning for printed books.

Thomas Matthews, former front desk guard, dies on May 15, one week before his 100th birthday (See 1963).

Linda Voigts conducts a seminar in Middle English Paleography, funded by the National Endowment for the Humanities.

The income from the Charles E. Mason, '05 Memorial Fund, established in 1981 by bequest of Fanny P. Mason, is assigned to the support of the Houghton Library. Barbara Wallace Grossman establishes a fund for the purchase of library materials for the Harvard Theatre Collection. The Francis W. Hatch, '19 Book Fund, established by his bequest in 1975, is augmented by his family and friends for acquisitions for the Harvard Theatre Collection. Franklin H. Kissner, '30 establishes the Franklin H. Kissner Fund for support of the Houghton Library. The Andrew Oliver, '28 Book Fund is established by the gift of Augustus P. Loring, '38, and added to by Mrs. Andrew Oliver and friends. The Thomas W. Streeter, '07 Fund is established by the gift of Augustus P. Loring and added to by Frank Streeter, '40, Henry S. Streeter, '42 and friends, in memory of Thomas W. Streeter. The Edmund L. Lincoln Fund for architectural bibliography is established. The Perry G. E. and Elizabeth W. Miller Fund is established for the Houghton Library. The William Henry Bond Book Fund for the purchase of books and manuscripts is established by members of the Library Visiting Committee and added to by many other friends of William H. Bond upon his retirement.

The Library receives an anonymous gift of

Lawrence Dowler.

$650,000 to help maintain services, special emphasis to be placed on support staff salaries.

EXHIBITIONS

Exhibition Room

Goethe

Printing Types through Five Centuries: An Exhibition Selected from the Bentinck-Smith Collection in the Department of Printing and Graphic Arts, for the Forty-fifth Reunion of the Class of 1937

An Exhibition of Music Manuscripts to Honor the Boston Symphony Orchestra

Decorated Papers: A Selection from the Loring Collection

Amy Lowell Room

Emerson

Louisa May Alcott

Amy Lowell: Acquisitions acquired through the Amy Lowell Fund

Widener Rotunda

German Illustrated Books of the Renaissance

The Golden Age of Printing in the Netherlands

Theodore Roosevelt Gallery

TR in Cartoon, 1908–1919: J. N. Donahey

From the Pforzheimer Library (celebrating its gift of books and manuscripts, 1981)

LECTURES

David McKitterick, "Educating a Paragon: Samuel Sandars and the Cambridge University Library." Fourteenth George Parker Winship Lecture. March 2, 1982.

James Laughlin, "A Portrait of Ezra Pound." Fifteenth George Parker Winship Lecture. May 5, 1982.

Rosamond McKitterick, "Early Medieval Libraries: Catalogues and Extant Books, 750–900." Sixteenth George Parker Winship Lecture. October 25, 1982.

William H. Bond, "Thomas Hollis's Emblematic Book Bindings." Seventeenth George Parker Winship Lecture. December 8, 1982.

CONCERTS

Emanuel Borok, violin; Michael Zaretsky, viola; Luise Vosgerchian, piano. Brahms. February 15, 1982.

The New World String Quartet. Haydn, Dvořák, and Beethoven. March 15, 1982.

Galimir String Quartet. Haydn, Webern, and Dvořák. October 14, 1982.

Joseph Silverstein, violin; Jules Eskin, cello; Gilbert Kalish, piano; Beethoven. November 21, 1982.

PUBLICATIONS

Bodoni Keepsake. Facsimile of Giambattista Bodoni's first type specimen, *Fregi e majuscole,* 1771. [Cambridge: The Houghton Library, 1982].

Roger E. Stoddard, *The Houghton Library, 1942–1982: A Fortieth Anniversary Exhibition.* Cambridge: The Houghton Library, 1982. Exhibition catalogue.

James E. Walsh and Eugene M. Weber, *Goethe.* Cambridge: Harvard College Library and the Goethe Institute of Boston, 1982. Exhibition catalogue.

Eleanor M. Garvey, "Printing Types through Five Centuries: An Exhibition Selected from the Bentinck-Smith Collections in the Department of Printing and Graphic Arts," *Harvard Library Bulletin,* 30 (1982), 349–354. Exhibition checklist.

1983

The Houghton Library and the Goethe Institute of Boston celebrate the sixty-fifth birthday of James E. Walsh, Keeper of Printed Books, with a festschrift. Gifts in honor of Mr. Walsh include a manuscript by Richard Beer-Hofmann, given by his daughter Miriam Beer-Hofmann Lens, and a *modus scribendi* from the Benedictine monastery of Melk, given by Philip Hofer.

Volume VII of the *BAL* (James Kirke Paulding to Frank Richard Stockton) is published in March.

The Theatre Collection acquires a cast aluminum model of the Universal Theatre of Friedrich Kiesler and a significant group of drawings by Al Hirschfeld, the gift of Melvin R. Seiden, '52.

Houghton begins machine cataloguing for printed books.

Beverly Wilson Palmer and her associates begin work on the papers of Charles Sumner; their catalogue and a microfilm of the papers will be published by Chadwyck-Healey in 1988.

Mrs. Donald F. Hyde is appointed Honorary Curator of Eighteenth-Century English Literature in the College Library.

Philip Hofer establishes a trust for acquisitions by the Department of Printing and Graphic Arts. The gift of Mrs. Russel Crouse is used to establish the Russel Crouse Fund for Twentieth Century Theatre in memory of her husband. The William Morris Hunt Book Fund for the Theatre Collection is established. John J. Slocum establishes the John J. Slocum, '36, Houghton Library Fund. Charles J. Tanenbaum, '34 establishes the Charles J. Tanenbaum Library Fund for the support of exhibitions in the Houghton Library. Willard B. Pope, '26 gives the Evelyn Ryan Pope Book Fund in memory of his wife for the purchase of rare books or manuscripts relating to John Keats or Benjamin Robert Haydon, and to the art and literature of their period. The Thomas Matthews Memorial Fund for the purchase of books is established by Mr. and Mrs. Charles A. Clarkson.

EXHIBITIONS

Exhibition Room

On the Shoulders of Giants: Galileo and Kepler to Newton

Are We Alone? The Idea of Intelligent Life in the Universe

Luther

Late Medieval and Renaissance Illuminated Manuscripts, 1350–1525

Collector's Choice: A Selection of Books and Manuscripts Given by Harrison D. Horblit to the Harvard College Library

Spanish and Portuguese Books and Manuscripts, Ninth–Twentieth Centuries

Hans Holbein as a Graphic Artist

Theatre Collection

The Universal Theatre of Friedrich Kiesler

The Harvard Theatre Collection Celebrates Al Hirschfeld

Widener Rotunda

Meditation, History, and Romance: A Selection of Medieval Literary Manuscripts from Macrobius to Dante

Theodore Roosevelt Gallery

From the Portfolio Collection

Roosevelt in Retirement: Photographs, 1909–19

Letters of Theodore Roosevelt

LECTURES

Eugene Weber, Rodney G. Dennis, Robert Spaethling; Roger E. Stoddard, moderator. Three talks on Goethe, in connection with the festschrift for James E. Walsh. Co-sponsored by the Goethe Institute of Boston. January 6, 1983.

Karl S. Guthke, "Are We Alone? The Idea of Intelligent Life in the Universe in Philosophy and Literature from Copernicus to H.G. Wells." Eighteenth George Parker Winship Lecture. March 9, 1983.

John Plummer, "Jean Poyet: A Recently Identified French Artist of the Fifteenth Century." Philip and Frances Hofer Lecture. April 25, 1983.

John Rowlands, "Hans Holbein the Younger as a Graphic Artist." Philip and Frances Hofer Lecture. October 15, 1983.

Owen Gingerich, "Copernicus's *De revolutionibus:* an Example of Renaissance Scientific Printing." Nineteenth George Parker Winship Lecture. Co-sponsored by the Bibliographical Society of America. November 14, 1983.

Paul Raabe, "Collections, Scholars, and Librarians at the Herzog August Bibliothek Wolfenbüttel." Twentieth

George Parker Winship Lecture.

John H. Blum, "Theodore Roosevelt." December 2, 1983. (Emerson Hall).

Steven Ozment, "The Reformation as an Intellectual Revolution." Twenty-first George Parker Winship Lecture. December 14, 1983.

CONCERTS

Doriot Anthony Dwyer, flute; Ikuko Mizuno, violin; Michael Zaretsky, viola; Ann Hobson Pilot, harp. Bach, Saint-Saëns, Reger, and Debussy. February 27, 1983.

Veronica Jochum, piano and the New World String Quartet. Brahms. April 7, 1983.

Leslie Amper and Randall Hodgkinson, pianists. Mozart, Stravinsky, and Rachmaninoff. October 31, 1983.

The New World String Quartet and Harold Wright, clarinet. Mendelssohn, Janáček, and Mozart. December 2, 1983.

PUBLICATIONS

Essays in Honor of James Edward Walsh on His Sixty-Fifth Birthday. Hugh Amory and Rodney G. Dennis, eds. Cambridge: The Goethe Institute of Boston and The Houghton Library, 1983.

Houghton Library Printed Books and Ephemera: A Guide to the Catalogues, Finding Lists and Special Files with a List of Uncatalogued Collections. Prepared by Hugh Amory. [Cambridge], 1983.

Rodney G. Dennis, "An Exhibition of Music Manuscripts in the Houghton Library Prepared to Honor the BSO," *Harvard Library Bulletin,* 31 (1983), 88–95.

James E. Walsh, *Luther 1483–1983.* Cambridge: Harvard College Library, 1983. Exhibition catalogue.

Roger S. Wieck, *Late Medieval and Renaissance Illuminated Manuscripts 1350–1525 in the Houghton Library.* Cambridge: Department of Printing and Graphic Arts, Harvard College Library, 1983. Exhibition catalogue.

Owen Gingerich, *Collector's Choice: A Selection of Books and Manuscripts Given by Harrison D. Horblit to the Harvard College Library.* Cambridge, 1983. Exhibition catalogue.

1984

The Moldenhauer Archives, a major collection of manuscripts, scores, letters and in some cases the entire estates of leading twentieth-century composers is a significant addition to the music materials held by the Houghton Library. This acquisition is made possible by generous gifts from Francis Goelet, '47 and many others.

The 200th anniversary of the death of Samuel Johnson is commemorated by a meeting of The Johnsonians, with an exhibition and talks at the Houghton Library. The exhibition and catalogue are prepared by five doctoral candidates in the English Department under the guidance of Roger E. Stoddard and Hugh Amory.

Eleanor Garvey conducts a workshop on "Drawings for Book Illustration" as part of a symposium on Old Master Drawings: Origin, Function, Technique at the Harvard University Art Museums.

Severe problems with leaks—including, at one point, the collapse of a portion of the ceiling in the Exhibition Room—lead to plans for a new roof, incorporating a neoprene sheet masked by slate shingles.

Franklin Haase Kissner is appointed Honorary Curator of Roman Books in the College Library. Frederick R. Koch is appointed Honorary Curator of Theatre Arts in the College Library. Hans Moldenhauer is appointed Honorary Curator of Twentieth Century Music in the College Library. Louis Krasner is appointed Honorary Curator of Music Manuscripts in the College Library.

Fernando Zóbel, Honorary Curator of Calligraphy in the Harvard College Library since 1969, dies in Rome on June 3.

Philip Hofer, Curator of Printing and Graphic Arts Emeritus and founder of the Department of Printing and Graphic Arts in the Houghton Library, dies on November 9.

Through a trust bequeathed by Phillips Barry, '01, the Phillips Barry Bequest is established, with one third of the income designated for the purchase of rare books and manuscripts. The gift of family and friends of Helen Willard is used to establish the Helen Delano Willard Memorial Fund for the Theatre Collection in her memory. Dr. David Crocker, '33 establishes the David Crocker Book Fund. Harrison D. Horblit, '33, establishes the Harrison D. Horblit Fund for books about books. Friends and associates of Philip Hofer launch a fund drive to endow the Philip Hofer Curatorship of Printing and Graphic Arts. The Hermon Dunlap Smith Bequest is used to establish a fund to be used for the purchase of books and maps. Melvin R. Seiden, '52 establishes the Melvin R. Seiden Library Fund to purchase drawings for the Harvard Theatre Collection.

EXHIBITIONS

Exhibition Room

The Dark Side of the Enlightenment

Drawings for Book Illustration: Selections from the Hofer Collection in the Houghton Library (concurrently with "Master Drawings and Watercolors: The Hofer Collection," at the Fogg Museum)

"He Has Long Outlived His Century": Books, drawings, and prints depicting the writings and influence of Dr. Samuel Johnson

Class of 1924 Exhibition

Marks in Books Shown and Explained

Musical Americana in Harvard Libraries

American Historical Autographs (In Honor of Oscar Handlin)

Amy Lowell Room

Pierre de Ronsard

Theatre Collection

An Exhibition Honoring Playwright Sidney Kingsley on the 50th Anniversary of His Pulitzer Prize for *Men in White*)

Longing for the Ideal: Images of Marie Taglioni and the Romantic Ballet

Widener Lobby

The Dreyfus Affair: A 90th Anniversary Exhibition (exhibition of Houghton material assembled by the Judaica Department).

Widener Rotunda

Rara Astronomica
Surrealism

Theodore Roosevelt Gallery

From the Postcard Collection
TR in March and Song, 1898–1919
Theodore Roosevelt in the Badlands, 1883–86

LECTURES

Roger E. Stoddard, "'Fidèle à nos Habitudes Laborieuses': Four Variations on a Theme by J.-C. Brunet." February 14, 1984.

Michael Parker, "History, Type and Technology." Co-sponsored by the Letterpress Guild of New England. February 22, 1984.

Henry Snyder, "How ESTC will Change the World of Research." April 25, 1984.

Hans Halbey, "Twentieth-Century Calligraphy in Germany." Philip and Frances Hofer Lecture. October 15, 1984.

Robert H. Taylor, "The Early Ineptitudes of a Collector." Twenty-second George Parker Winship Lecture. October 18, 1984.

Sue Allen, "Nineteenth-Century American Book Covers." Twenty-third George Parker Winship Lecture. November 5, 1984.

Edwin Binney, 3rd, "The Many Faces of Marie Taglioni." Harvard Theatre Collection. November 7, 1984.

Konrad Oberhuber, "Hofer Drawings." November 14, 1984.

I Bernard Cohen, "The Newtonian Revolution and Its Significance." Twenty-fourth George Parker Winship Lecture. November 27, 1984.

Three talks on Samuel Johnson: James Engell, "His Inhibitions"; David D. Perkins, "His Influence on Modern Poets"; and Sidney E. Ives, "His Wit and Humor." December 14, 1984.

CONCERTS

Gustav Leonhardt, harpsichord and clavichord. Balbastre, C.P.E. Bach, W. Fr. Bach, and J.S. Bach. February 21, 1984.

Bethany Beardslee, soprano and the Atlantic String Quartet. Schubert, Schoenberg, and Berg. April 2, 1984.

Emanuel Borok and Vyacheslav Uritsky, violins; Michael Zaretsky, viola. Mozart, Martinů, Dvořák, and Kodály. November 2, 1984.

Veronica Jochum, piano. Clara Wieck, Robert Schumann, Clara Schumann and Brahms. December 7, 1984.

PUBLICATIONS

F. Thomas Noonan, *Houghton Library: The Collection and Reading Room.* Cambridge: Harvard College Library, 1984.

F. Thomas Noonan, *The Dark Side of the Enlightenment.* Cambridge: Harvard College Library, 1984. Exhibition catalogue.

He Has Long Outlived His Century. Catalogue of an exhibition of books and manuscripts collected by Mary and Donald Hyde, Arthur A. Houghton, Jr., Robert Metzdorf, Amy Lowell, Harold Murdock, Houghton Mifflin Co., and others. Cambridge, The Houghton Library, 1984.

Stanley J. Kahrl, C. Walter Hodges, David Bevington and Jeanne T. Newlin, S*hakespeare's First Globe Theatre: The Harvard Theatre Collection Model Designed by C. Walter Hodges.* Cambridge: Harvard Theatre Collection, Harvard College Library, 1984. Second edition.

Edwin Binney, 3rd, *Longing for the Ideal: Images of Marie Taglioni in the Romantic Ballet.* Cambridge: Harvard Theatre Collection, Harvard College Library, 1984. Exhibition catalogue.

1985

Funded by the National Endowment for the Humanities, the Solidarity Bibliographic Center at Harvard, a cooperative project to help organize, preserve and give access to documentation from Solidarity and other independent Polish sources, begins operation in January 1985. The project will remain in the Houghton Library until 1991.

James Lewis is appointed Curator of the Reading Room, succeeding F. Thomas Noonan.

Rodney G. Dennis and Roger Stoddard begin teaching Medieval Studies 105, the Produc-

tion of Manuscripts and Printed Books Before 1600 (still offered in 1992).

Larry Dowler, James Walsh and Roger Stoddard accompany Vol. II of the Gutenberg Bible to the University of California at Davis where the printing inks are analyzed using the cyclotron. Work proceeds without interruption around the clock, with Houghton staff members standing four-hour shifts to supervise the handling of the book.

"Theatre of Marvels," a major exhibition in the Theatre Collection devoted to popular entertainment, is drawn from the Marian Hannah Winter Memorial Collection.

"Artists of the Book in Boston, 1890–1910," a major exhibition by Nancy Finlay, is funded by the National Endowment for the Arts.

The Houghton Library is the principal lender to the exhibition "Edward Lear, 1812–1888" at the Royal Academy of Arts in London. The exhibition is subsequently shown at the National Academy of Design in New York. Over one hundred items from the Houghton Library, originally the gifts of William B. Osgood Field and Philip Hofer, are included in the catalogue by Vivien Noakes.

A portrait of Paula Beer-Hofmann is the first portrait of a woman to hang in the Reading Room.

Richard C. Marcus, '60 gives an endowment to the Theatre Collection to be used for the acquisition of historical materials as they become available and to process and preserve them and other valuable items in the collection. The Rose Winter and Marian Hannah Winter Fund is established by bequest of Marian Winter for acquisitions in the Harvard Theatre Collection and to the Winter Memorial Collection. G. Barry Bingham, Sr., '28 establishes the Barry Bingham, Sr. Publication Fund for the Harvard Theatre Collection. The Stanley Marcus Endowment for Rare Books in the Houghton Library is established by Nonesuch Corporation on behalf of Stanley Marcus, '25, to be used for processing, preserving, and acquiring unique materials.

EXHIBITIONS

Exhibition Room

Increase Mather and Seventeenth-Century New England

Twenty Years of German Collection Building, 1966–86
Spanish and Portuguese Sixteenth-Century Books
Gifts from the Class of 1925
Thoreau
Artists of the Book in Boston, 1890–1910

Amy Lowell Room

Thoreau

Theatre Collection

Theatre of Marvels

Widener Rotunda

A Fear of Love: D. H. Lawrence, 1885–1930
Selections from the Library of Harry Elkins Widener
Thomas Dudley

Theodore Roosevelt Gallery

TR in Cartoons: John T. McCutcheon
A Cartoon Biography of Theodore Roosevelt

LECTURES

Edwin Wolf 2nd, "On Colonial American Book Collections." Co-sponsored by Mather House (with other lectures by Peter J. Gomes, Robert Middlekauf, and Mason Lowance, 11–13 February) in connection with the Mather exhibition. February 14, 1985.

Arno Werner, "Judging A Book by Its Cover: The History and Development of Bookbinding." Lecture and demonstration co-sponsored with the Lettering Arts Guild of Boston. March 14, 1985.

Arthur Freeman, "John Payne Collier and the Contagion of Forgery." Twenty-fifth George Parker Winship Lecture. April 24, 1985.

Anne Anninger, "Early Spanish and Portuguese Illustrated Books." May 30, 1985.

Sue Allen, Nancy Finlay, Max Hall, James F. O'Gorman, and Betty Smith. Symposium on "Artists of the Book in Boston, 1890–1910." October 30, 1985.

Karl S. Guthke, "B. Traven, or Was It Somebody Else? Towards a Solution of 'The Greatest Literary Mystery of Modern Times.'"Twenty-sixth George Parker Winship Lecture. November 12, 1985.

Susan Otis Thompson, "Publishing for the Parlor: Thomas Bird Mosher and Elbert Hubbard." Philip and Frances Hofer Lecture. November 21, 1985.

CONCERTS

Dawn Upshaw, soprano and Earl Kim, piano; Hiroshi C. Shibutani, flute; Virginia Haines, viola; Gillian Benet, harp. *Lieder* by Schumann, Mahler, Berg, Kim, and Schubert. February 8, 1985.

Ralph Gomberg, oboe and the New World String Quartet. Stamitz, Kirchner, Mozart, and Beethoven. April 12, 1985.

Malcolm Lowe, violin; Jules Eskin, cello; Gilbert Kalish, piano. Scarlatti, Ravel, and Brahms. October 25, 1985.

The Lydian String Quartet. Mozart, Bartók, and Brahms. December 7, 1985.

PUBLICATIONS

Anne Anninger, *Spanish and Portuguese Sixteenth-Century Books in the Department of Printing and Graphic Arts.* Cambridge: Harvard College Library, 1985. Exhibition catalogue.

Jean Evans, *Alphabet.* [1985].

Roger E. Stoddard, *Marks in Books, Illustrated and Explained.* Cambridge: The Houghton Library, Harvard University, 1985. Exhibition catalogue.

Nancy Finlay, *Artists of the Book in Boston, 1890–1910.* Cambridge: Department of Printing and Graphic Arts, The Houghton Library, Harvard College Library, 1985. Exhibition catalogue.

James E. Walsh (ed.), *German and Austrian Drama: A Guide to the Microfilm Collection of German and Austrian plays in the Houghton Library.* Woodbridge, Connecticut: Research Publications, 1985.

Rodney G. Dennis, *Houghton Library: Manuscripts and Drawings. A Handlist of Finding Aids with a List of the Published Guides.* [Cambridge: The Houghton Library], 1985.

Theatre of Marvels: Popular Entertainments on Boulevard and Fairground. Cambridge: Harvard Theatre Collection, Harvard College Library, 1985. Exhibition catalogue.

1986

The Manuscript Survey and Guide Project, directed by Lofton Wilson from the Houghton Library, creates machine-readable bibliographic records for 5,000 manuscript collections in more than fifty repositories at Harvard and Radcliffe. The project is funded primarily by a grant from the National Historical Publications and Records Commission.

Roger Stoddard, Katharine F. Pantzer and other staff members collectively continue teaching W. H. Bond's course, English 296, Descriptive and Analytical Bibliography. Use of the Houghton seminar room by other faculty members is also on the increase. In the spring semester, the seminar room accommodates nineteen special meetings of classes not regularly held in the Library, given by ten professors and instructors in the Faculty of Arts and Sciences, the School of Design, and the Divinity School. Subjects include English and American literature, history, classics, the fine arts, and romance languages.

Medieval Studies 107, a general paleography course taught by Paul Meyvaert and Rodney G.

Dennis for one semester, introduces a series of paleography workshops offered in subsequent years: Latin Paleography, 1200–1400, taught by Prof. R. J. Tarrant; Latin and Vernacular Hands of the Italian Renaissance, taught by Prof. James Hankins; English Handwriting, 1550–1650, taught by Rodney G. Dennis; German Handwriting, 1500–1650, taught by Prof. Steven Ozment; German Handwriting, 1700–1900, by Prof. Karl S. Guthke; and French Handwriting, 1500–1600, by Prof. Donald Stone.

James Walsh, Roger Stoddard and Dennis Marnon accompany Vol. I of the Gutenberg Bible to the University of California at Davis for examination by cyclotron (See above, 1985).

After numerous revisions, Volume I of the *STC* is published in May.

Chadwyck-Healey publishes the main Houghton manuscript catalogue, in ten volumes. James E. Walsh resigns as head of cataloguing, after 35 years, to work on *A Catalogue of Fifteenth-Century Printed Books in the Harvard University Library*. He is succeeded by Mollie Della Terza. The National Endowment for the Humanities awards the first of two grants for a catalogue of Medieval and Renaissance manuscripts in the Houghton Library by Laura Light.

He Has Long Outlived His Century receives first place in the Katharine Kyes Leab and Daniel L. Leab "American Book Prices Current" Exhibition Catalogue Awards for 1986. *Artists of the Book in Boston, 1890–1910* by Nancy Finlay and *The Dark Side of the Enlightenment* by F. Thomas Noonan receive honorable mention. *Marks in Books, Illustrated and Explained* receives the Blue Ribbon for Design in the New England Book Show.

G. Barry Bingham, Sr., '28 is appointed Honorary Curator of Modern Drama in the College Library.

William Bentinck-Smith, '37 establishes the Hofer-Holyoke Fund in support of the Philip Hofer Curatorship of Printing and Graphic Arts. Melvin R. Seiden, '52 establishes an acquisitions fund for the Department of Printing and Graphic Arts in honor of Frank Denny. Stanley J. Kahrl, '53 establishes the George and Faith Kahrl Fund for Theatre History in honor of his parents. Arthur A. Houghton, Jr., '29 establishes the Arthur A. Houghton, Jr. Fund.

EXHIBITIONS

Exhibition Room

Latin Verse of the Renaissance
Re-conceiving Women's Books: The Emergence of a Feminist Perspective within Male Cultures from Plato to Evelyn Keller
Baroque Rome: Maps, plans and views of the city from the collection of Franklin H. Kissner
Fiftieth Class Reunion: Loans from the Private Collections of James Laughlin and John J. Slocum
Danish Literature: Saxo Grammaticus to Isak Dinesen
Manuscripts by Harvard Authors
Randolph Caldecott, 1846–86
John Eliot, 1604–90: An Exhibition of Books and Manuscripts to Celebrate Founder's Day, Roxbury Latin School
Twenty Years of German Collection Building, 1966–86

Amy Lowell Room

An Exhibition of Manuscripts Relating to the Pastorate of Thomas Shepard at the First Church in Cambridge, 1636–49
Pierre de Ronsard, 1524–85

Mollie Della Terza. *Photo by Diane Asséo Griliches.*

Roger E. Stoddard's office. *Photo by Diane Asséo Griliches.*

Widener Rotunda

Halley's Comet and Others

Russian Constructivist Graphic Design

Isak Dinesen: From the Collection of Parmenia Migel Ekstrom

Theodore Roosevelt Gallery

TR and Books: Just Beyond the Title-page

Theodore and Alice: A Harvard Romance (celebrating a gift of letters of Roosevelt and his first wife Alice Hathaway Lee by their great-granddaughter, Joanna Sturm)

Theodore and Edith: Centennial of a Marriage (celebrating the gift of papers of Roosevelt's second wife Edith Kermit Carow and their daughter Ethel Roosevelt Derby by her daughters, Edith Derby Williams and Sarah Alden Derby Gannett)

LECTURES

D. F. McKenzie, "Signs of Sense? Bibliography and the Sociology of Texts." Twenty-seventh George Parker Winship Lecture. January 28, 1986.

R. J. Tarrant, Jan M. Ziolkowski, Wendell V. Clausen, Dante M. Della Terza. Symposium on Latin Poetry of the Renaissance. February 6, 1986.

Susan Moller Okin, Ruth Perry, Barbara Walzer, Barbara Haber, and Marsha Jean Darling. Lectures on the Women's Books exhibition. March 3, 19, 27, and April 4, 1986.

Anthony Crane, "Walter Crane and Frederick Sandys: A Grandson's View of Two Victorian Artists." Philip and Frances Hofer Lecture. April 3, 1986.

Adrian and Joyce Lancaster Wilson, "A Medieval Mirror: *Speculum humanae salvationis* 1324–1500." Twenty-eighth George Parker Winship Lecture. April 15, 1986.

Margaret Maloney, "Limed Twigs to Catch Young Birds." Twenty-ninth George Parker Winship Lecture. May 5, 1986.

Michael Winship, "Hermann Ernst Ludewig, America's Forgotten Bibliographer." Thirtieth George Parker Winship Lecture. September 24, 1986. Later published as a Malkin Lecture by the Columbia Library School.

Sven H. Rossel, "Fantasy and Reality: A Thematic Foray into Danish Literature." November 3, 1986.

Lance Hidy, "Low Brow, High Minded." November 13, 1986.

Ludvig Holberg, "Bringing Theatre and 'Moral Thoughts' Home to Denmark." With a Talk by Nancy S. Reinhardt. November 19, 1986.

John E. Benson, "Carved Letters from the John Stevens Shop." Philip and Frances Hofer Lecture. December 4, 1986.

Oscar Handlin, "Learned Books and Revolutionary Action, 1776." Thirty-first George Parker Winship Lecture. December 10, 1986. Later published in the *Harvard Library Bulletin,* v. 34.

CONCERTS

Paul O'Dette, lute. Lute music by Joan Ambrosio Dalza, Francesco da Milano, Philip van Wilder, Daniell Bachelar, Edward Collard, William Byrd, John Johnson, and John Dowland. February 19, 1986.

The New World String Quartet. Haydn, Verdi, and Schumann. April 4, 1986.

The New World String Quartet, with Michael Zaretsky, viola and Bruce Coppock, cello. Schubert, Schoenberg, Beethoven. October 31, 1986.

Christopher Trakas, baritone and Steven Blier, piano. Schubert, *Die Winterreise.* December 12, 1986.

PUBLICATIONS

Nancy S. Reinhardt, *Danish Literature: Saxo Grammaticus to Isak Dinesen.* Cambridge: Harvard College Library, 1986. Exhibition catalogue.

Rodney G. Dennis, *Manuscripts by Harvard Authors.* Catalogue of an exhibition at the Houghton Library to celebrate the 350th Anniversary of the Founding of Harvard College Library. Cambridge, 1986.

A Catalogue of Manuscripts in the Houghton Library. 8 v. + 2 v. of microfiches. Alexandria, Va.: Chadwyck-Healey, 1986.

Poemata Humanistica Decem. Ed. Rodney G. Dennis. [Harvard College Library], 1986. Renaissance Latin poems with English translations by friends of the Houghton Library.

Nancy Finlay, *Randolph Caldecott, 1846–1886. A Checklist of the Caroline Miller Parker Collection in the Houghton Library.* Cambridge: Department of Printing and Graphic Arts, The Houghton Library, Harvard College Library, 1986.

1987

William H. Bond is appointed Librarian, Emeritus, after he retires from teaching. He is also appointed Professor of Bibliography, Emeritus.

Problems with the heating and air-conditioning system reach a crisis with black charcoal dust spraying from the air circulation vents. On January 8, a quantity of moisture and steam enters the mezzanine, first floor and ground floor office levels, forcing the evacuation of the Reading Room. Only prompt action by staff prevents damage to framed items hanging on the walls of affected office areas.

During the summer, asbestos is removed from the ceiling of the Reading Room and new lighting fixtures are installed. Additional electrical outlets are installed to facilitate the ever-increasing use of laptop computers by research-ers. While this work is being done, the Exhibition Room is used as a temporary reading room to avoid any interruption in services to researchers, and the air quality in the building is continuously monitored by Environmental Health and Safety.

Thirty-eight drawings by Edward Lear are filmed by Bayerischer Rundfunk for use in a public television program on "Edward Lear in Corsica," part of a series on artists' travels.

Marks in Books, Illustrated and Explained receives first prize in the 2nd division from the American Library Association, ACRL Rare Books and Manuscripts Section.

Major acquisitions include papers of Rudolf Kolisch, William Empson and John Ashbery. In April, Eric Offenbacher presents to the Library the only surviving autograph leaf of Mozart's *Sinfonia Concertante,* K. 364/320d.

Melvin R. Seiden, '52 establishes an acquisitions fund for the Department of Printing and Graphic Arts in honor of William Bentinck-Smith; another in honor of Eleanor Garvey; and the Philip Hofer Prize Fund for student book collectors and print collectors. The bequest of Betty B. McAndrew is used to establish the Betty B. McAndrew Book Fund for the Department of Printing and Graphic Arts. The Jay M. Pasachoff, '63 and Naomi Pasachoff, '68 Book Fund is established for the acquisition of astronomy books. The Elizabeth K. Sabsay Bequest is established for the Houghton Library. Colleagues and students of Eugene M. Weber establish a book fund in his memory, to be used for the purchase of German books. The Susan Bennett Fund is established by the Brattle Foundation for the purchase of materials for the Department of Printing and Graphic Arts.

EXHIBITIONS

Exhibition Room

New Books by Fielding (concurrent with "The Virgin and the Witch," at the Law School)

John Updike: The Art of Adding and the Art of Taking Away

William Dean Howells

Class of 1937 Exhibition

Pushkin and his Friends: The Making of a Literature and a Myth

Randolph Caldecott

Amy Lowell Room

Jane Austen
Chaucer
Thomas Wolfe

Ground Floor

Early Animals and Writers about Animals, for the Fourteenth New England Medieval Conference

Theatre Collection

The Stage Designs of Leo Kerz
Four Hundred Years of Dance Notation
Dressing Broadway: The Costume Designs of Lucinda
Ballard

Widener Memorial Rooms

English Romantic Poets: Meetings and Correspondences

Theodore Roosevelt Gallery

Theodore Roosevelt: Imagery for a Presidency
TR in Cartoon: The Art of Joseph Keppler
Theodore Roosevelt: Traveling Journalist

Law School

The Virgin and the Witch (prepared by Hugh Amory)

LECTURES

Ruthe R. Battestin, Martin C. Battestin, Susan Staves, and
Robert Alter; James Engell, moderator. Henry Fielding
Symposium. January 14 and 15, 1987.
John Bidwell, "Hiring, Firing and Factory Discipline in an
Early American Paper Mill." Thirty-second George
Parker Winship Lecture. March 2, 1987.
Warner Berthoff, Elizabeth A. Falsey, and John Updike;
William Alfred, moderator. "John Updike Manuscripts:
Three Talks Suggested by the Exhibition at the Hough-
ton Library." March 11, 1987.
Roland John Wiley and Ann Hutchinson Guest, "Aspects
of Dance Notation." Theatre Collection. March 1987.
David McKitterick, "The Young Geoffrey Keynes: A Bib-
liophile Turns Bibliographer." April 6, 1987.
Meir Shalev, "Rewriting History in the Bible." Max and
Celia Leavitt Memorial Lecture. April 29, 1987.
John Updike, "William Dean Howells." Co-sponsored by
the William Dean Howells Memorial Committee, in
connection with the Howells exhibition. May 1, 1987.
Published in the *New Yorker* and in pamphlet form by
the William Dean Howells Memorial Committee.
Mirjam M. Foot, "Bookbinding and the History of Books."
Philip and Frances Hofer Lecture. May 7, 1987.
Keith Maslen, "An Eighteenth-Century London Printer
and His Clients: Wm. Bowyer, Father and Son." Wid-
ener Memorial Room. September 10, 1987.
Robert Darnton, "The Science of Piracy: Illegal Publish-
ing in Eighteenth-Century France." Thirty-third George
Parker Winship Lecture. October 29, 1987.
Alessandro Corubolo and Gino Castiglioni, "Two Very
Private Printers of Verona." Philip and Frances Hofer
Lecture. November 14, 1987.

Richard Landon, "The Outcast Prophet and Other Tales
of Rarity from the True North." Thirty-fourth George
Parker Winship Lecture. November 18, 1987.

CONCERTS

Joel Krosnick, cello and Gilbert Kalish, piano. Beethoven,
and George Perle. January 23, 1987.
The New York Consort of Viols. Works for viols, by Gib-
bons, Purcell, Palestrina, David Loeb, Tison Street, and
others. April 6, 1987.
Reinhard Goebel, violin and Robert Hill, harpsichord. Von
Biber, Handel, Bach, and Veracini. November 2, 1987.
Dorothea Brinkmann, contralto; John McDonald, piano;
Michael Zaretsky, viola. Songs by Cornelius, Brahms,
Siegmeister, and Ives. December 14, 1987.

PUBLICATIONS

Henry Fielding, *An Institute of the Pleas of the Crown.*
Cambridge: The Houghton Library, 1987. Exhibition
keepsake.
Hugh Amory, *New Books by Fielding: Commentary Toward
an Exhibition.* Cambridge: The Houghton Library, 1987.
Exhibition catalogue.
Elizabeth A. Falsey, *The Art of Adding and The Art of Tak-
ing Away. Selections from John Updike's Manuscripts.*
Cambridge: Harvard College Library, 1987. Exhibition
catalogue.
John E. Malmstad and William Mills Todd, III, *Pushkin
and his Friends: The Making of a Literature and a Myth.*
[Cambridge]: The Houghton Library, 1987. Exhibition
catalogue.
Newlin, Jeanne T. (ed.), Martha R. Mahard and Robin L.
Baker, *Shakespeare Promptbooks in the Harvard Theatre
Collection: A Catalogue.* Special Issue of the *Harvard
Library Bulletin,* Winter, 1987.
Four Hundred Years of Dance Notation. Cambridge: Har-
vard Theatre Collection, Harvard College Library, 1987.
Exhibition catalogue.
Dressing Broadway: Costume Designs of Lucinda Ballard.
Cambridge: Harvard Theatre Collection, Harvard Col-
lege Library, 1987. Exhibition catalogue.
[Michael Anesko], *William Dean Howells, 1837–1920: A
Sesquicentennial Exhibition.* [Cambridge]: The Hough-
ton Library, 1987.

1988

"An Exhibition of the Philip Hofer
Bequest" celebrates Hofer's final legacy
to the Depart-ment of Printing and
Graphic Arts which he founded in 1938
and of which he was curator from 1938 to
1968. Melvin R. Seiden and Willi-am
Bentinck-Smith announce their successful
drive to fund the Philip Hofer curatorship
at the opening dinner.

A joint exhibition of "Sources for Twentieth-

Century Music" with a bilingual catalogue is on view at the Houghton Library and the Bayerische Staatsbibliothek in Munich. This is the culmination of a year-long effort to acquire twentieth-century music manuscripts and a fund-raising drive in which the Director of the University Library, the Chairman of the Music Department and the Houghton Library acted as partners, the first collaboration of this kind. An offshoot of this effort has been the formation in 1987 of the Bavaria-Harvard Commission for Twentieth-Century Music History, comprised of three scholars from Germany and three from Harvard and chaired by Rodney G. Dennis. "The Houghton Waltzes," a composition by Jerome Cohen based on melodies in the Strauss sketchbook in the Library, is performed at the exhibition opening.

"Impossible Picturesqueness: Edward Lear's Indian Watercolours, 1873–1875," a loan show from the Department of Printing and Graphic Arts, is on view at the Miriam and Ira D. Wallach Art Gallery, Columbia University, New York, from October 19 to December 3. The exhibition is documented in a catalogue by Vidja Dehejia with an essay by Allen Staley.

Many vellum codexes are threatened with damage when the climate control systems of Houghton and Pusey fail during a heat wave. The Manuscript Department undertakes a project to house all early vellum codexes in individual cases.

Beginning in June, the Reading Room is open Saturdays from 9:00 to 1:00, as well as from Monday through Friday 9:00 to 5:00. The library was originally open on Saturday, but had been forced to eliminate Saturday hours due to budgetary restrictions. The Harvard Extension School provides the funds for the extra staff to make the library available for their students.

English 296z, An Introduction to Codicology, taught by Rodney G. Dennis, and English 296w, taught by Roger Stoddard, alternate with Medieval Studies 105 (see 1985).

Roger Stoddard and other members of the Houghton staff participate with Gino Lee and James Barondess in teaching Adams 114: The Art and History of the Printed Word. In sessions at the Houghton Library, students study

the evolution of typography and layout from original examples from the Library's collections. In studio sessions at The Bow and Arrow Press, they learn the techniques of letterpress printing and produce several typographic projects (see 1980).

The Philip Hofer Prize in Collecting is offered for the first time. Winners are William Bikales, of the Graduate School in Economics, with a collection of modern literary first editions, and Adam Weiss, '89, with a collection of contemporary prints and paintings. Honorable mention goes to Michael Choi, '91 and Robert O'Hara, GSAS.

Katharine F. Pantzer is awarded the Gold Medal of the Bibliographical Society for outstanding contributions, the second woman and the sixth American among the 27 recipients to date.

Parmenia Migel Ekstrom is appointed Honorary Curator of Ballet in the Harvard College Library.

Joseph S. Stern, Jr., '40 establishes the Joseph S. Stern, Jr. Fund for the Department of Printing and Graphic Arts for acquisitions. Income from the John R. McGinley, '31 Bequest, established in 1987, is assigned to the Houghton Library.

EXHIBITIONS

Exhibition Room

Five Centuries of Books and Manuscripts in Modern Greek

The Bible in the Twelfth Century: An Exhibition of Manuscripts

Edward Lear as a Book Illustrator

Fiftieth Reunion Exhibition: Gifts of books and manuscripts by members of the Class of 1938, including E. Hyde Cox, the late Augustus P. Loring, and Crocker Wight

Sources for Twentieth-Century Music History

The Philip Hofer Bequest to the Department of Printing and Graphic Arts

The Magnetized Observer: Hawthorne's Romantic Vision (Joint exhibition with the Essex Institute)

Amy Lowell Room

The Two Emmas: Jane Austen and Gustave Flaubert as seen through manuscripts and first editions of *Emma* and *Madame Bovary*

A Selection of Thomas Wolfe Manuscripts, for the publication of David Donald's Biography

A Selection of T. S. Eliot Books and Manuscripts, on the occasion of a talk by Donald C. Gallup

Theatre Collection

Shakespeare Promptbooks in the Harvard Theatre Collection

By Popular Demand: Theatrical Art of Al Hirschfeld, from the Melvin R. Seiden Gift

Widener Rotunda

Creating the Empire of Reason: Massachusetts Ratifies the United States Constitution, 1788

Writings by the Class of 1938

Francis J. Child, Lady Isabel and the Elf-Knight

An Exhibition of Works by Six New Englanders: from the Widener Room Collection

New Sweden and the Harvard College Library, 1638–1988—Early Settlers, Visitors and Influential Books

Theodore Roosevelt Gallery

On the Road with Theodore Roosevelt: American Crowd Scenes

LECTURES

R. J. Tarrant, Giles Constable, Richard Rouse and Ian Ziolkowski. Symposium on Manuscripts in the Twelfth Century. February 25, 1988. Later published in the *Harvard Library Bulletin,* n.s. 1, no. 3 (1990).

Albi Rosenthal, "Autograph Collecting from Goethe to Stefan Zweig." Co-sponsored by the Harvard Music Department. March 15, 1988.

Felix de Maréz Oyens, "Medieval Books at Auction: Crevenna, Röver, Meerman, and other Dutch Sales." Thirty-fifth George Parker Winship Lecture. March 31, 1988.

Anne Goldgar, "Getting Published in the Eighteenth Century," and Thomas Jay Siegel, "Using the Harvard Library in the Eighteenth and Twentieth Centuries." April 18, 1988.

Vivien Noakes, "Edward Lear: The Illustrator." Philip and Frances Hofer Lecture. May 5, 1988.

Donald C. Gallup, "The Eliots and the T. S. Eliot Collection at Harvard." Thirty-sixth George Parker Winship Lecture. October 17, 1988. Later published in the *Harvard Library Bulletin,* v. 36.

William Bentinck-Smith, Lucien Goldschmidt, Charles Ryskamp, Arthur Vershbow, "Philip Hofer as a Collector." Philip and Frances Hofer Lecture. Moderated by William H. Bond. November 10, 1988.

Patricia Meyer Spacks, "Boredom: The Two Emmas." Jointly sponsored by the Friends of the Harvard College Library and the Jane Austen Society of North America. November 13, 1988.

Karl S. Guthke, "Last Words: A Convention in Life, Literature and Biography." Thirty-seventh George Parker Winship Lecture. December 8, 1988.

Rodney G. Dennis, "The World of Madness and the World of Dreams: Charles Sumner and Philip Hofer as Collectors of Early Manuscripts." December 13, 1988. Later published in the *Grolier Library Gazette.*

CONCERTS

Ida Kavafian, violin; Steven Tenenbom, viola; Fred Sherry, cello. Ravel, Schoenberg, and Beethoven. February 17, 1988.

The New World String Quartet. Haydn, Bartók, and Beethoven. April 6, 1988.

A concert of works by Berg, Schoenberg, and Johann Strauss, in association with the Sources for Twentieth-Century Music History Exhibition. October 17, 1988. Co-sponsored by the Harvard Music Department and the University Library.

Malcolm Bilson, fortepiano. Haydn and Mozart. October 24, 1988.

The Muir String Quartet. Beethoven, Danielpour, and Kreisler. December 7, 1988.

PUBLICATIONS

Eleanor M. Garvey, Nancy Finlay, Rodney G. Dennis, and others. *A Catalogue of an Exhibition of the Philip Hofer Bequest in the Department of Printing and Graphic Arts.* Cambridge: Harvard College Library, 1988. Exhibition catalogue.

Helmut Hell, Sigrid von Moisy and Barbara Wolff, *Sources for Twentieth-Century Music History.* Catalogue of a joint exhibition of the Houghton Library and the Bayerische Staatsbibliothek. Munich and Cambridge, 1988.

Creating the Empire of Reason: Massachusetts Ratifies the United States Constitution. Cambridge: Harvard College Library, 1988. Exhibition catalogue.

Philip Hofer as a Collector. A symposium in conjunction with the exhibition of the Philip Hofer bequest to the Department of Printing and Graphic Arts. [Cambridge]: The Houghton Library, Harvard University, 1988.

Patrick K. Miehe, *The Robert Lowell Papers at the Houghton Library, Harvard University: A Guide to the Collection.* New York, 1990.

Laura Light, *The Bible in the Twelfth Century.* Cambridge: Harvard College Library, 1988. Exhibition catalogue.

Nancy S. Reinhardt, *New Sweden and the Harvard College Library, 1636–1986.* [Cambridge, 1988].

William H. Bond (ed.), *Letters from Thomas Hollis of Lincoln's Inn to Andrew Elliot.* Cambridge: The Houghton Library, 1988.

1989

Richard Wendorf becomes Librarian of the Houghton Library.

"An Exhibition of the Philip Hofer Bequest" travels to the Grolier Club in New York, where it is on view from September 12 through December 22. Associated events include lectures by Eleanor Garvey, Curator of Printing and Graphic Arts, and Rodney G. Dennis, Curator of Manuscripts.

Major acquisitions include the entire archives of Little Brown; the papers of Marguerite
Yourcenar, a bequest; the third and final install-
ment of John Ashbery's papers (during Ashbery's tenure as C. E. Norton Lecturer); and the
journals of John Cheever and the correspondence of Victoria Ocampo.

Arthur E. Vershbow and Charlotte Z. Vershbow are appointed Honorary Curators of Illustrated Books in the College Library.

The gift of Gifford Coombs, '80, is used to
establish the Gifford Coombs Book Fund. Gifts
from family, friends and alumni establish the
Henry E. Schniewind, '33 Memorial Book
Fund for the Department of Printing and
Graphic Arts.

EXHIBITIONS

Exhibition Room

Edward Lear's Indian Landscapes, 1873–1875

The First Roman Printers and the Idioms of Humanism

Fiftieth Reunion Exhibition: Manuscripts of Robert Lowell, A.B. 1939

The Great Adventurer: Theodore Roosevelt on Four Con-
tinents

Presentazione della Chinea

First Impressions: Printing in Cambridge, 1639–1989
(jointly with the Law School)

Photographs from the Collection of Harrison D. Horblit
(part of a university-wide exhibition on "The Invention
of Photography and Its Impact on Learning")

Nature in the New World

Amy Lowell Room

C. S. Peirce Papers, a Selection

Italian Humanists in Ten Manuscripts from the Houghton Library (for the meeting of the Renaissance Society
of America)

Selections from the Trotsky Papers

Lionel Feininger: A Selection from the Photographs presented by T. Lux Feininger

The Bible, An Exhibition Prepared for English 13

William Blake

Richard Wendorf. *Photo by Diane Asséo Griliches.*

Theatre Collection

Twenty-fifth Anniversary of the Boston Ballet
Commencement Exhibition: Students on Stage
The Stage Art of Theodore Komisarjevsky
Mirror to Nature: Portrait Daguerreotypes in the Harvard
    Theatre Collection
Under the Christmas Tree: Theatrical Toys for Girls and
    Boys

Widener Rotunda

El Gaucho y el Libro: Argentine Books from the Press of
    Francisco A. Colombo, 1922–66
Music Manuscripts from the Houghton Library

Theodore Roosevelt Gallery

Family Album: The Roosevelts at Home

LECTURES

Thomas Anfält, "The Enlightenment comes to Leufsta,
    Sweden: Carl de Geer, Industrialist, Savant, and Book
    Collector." February 15, 1989. Later published in the *Book
    Collector.*
D. F. McKenzie, "Speaking It or Printing It: Was It a
    Seventeenth-Century Problem?" March 21, 1989.
David McKitterick, "The Date as Token: A New Look at
    the Beginnings of the Cambridge University Press, 1570–
    1584." April 13, 1989.
Lilian Armstrong, "From Miniature to Woodcut: Venetian
    Book Decoration at the End of the Fifteenth Century."
    April 18, 1989.
William H. Scheide, "How a Library Came to Music
    Making." Thirty-eighth George Parker Winship Lecture,
    co-sponsored by the Harvard Music Department. May
    4, 1989.
William Alfred, A reading of poems by Robert Lowell. May
    9, 1989.
Tweed Roosevelt, "TR in Africa." A Benefit for the The-
    odore Roosevelt Collection Endowment. September 14,
    1989.
Eugenia Parry Janis, "Sir Thomas Phillipps: Photograph-
    ic Memoirs of a 'Vellomaniac.'" Philip and Frances Hofer
    Lecture. November 6, 1989.
Nicolas Barker, "Pietro Bizari and William Parry: The
    Perils of Authorship in the Sixteenth Century." Thirty-
    ninth George Parker Winship Lecture. November 16,
    1989.
August Heckscher, "The Printer's Challenge." Philip and
    Frances Hofer Lecture. November 29, 1989.

CONCERTS

James Buswell, violin; Leslie Parnas, cello, Lee Luvisi, pi-
    ano. Beethoven, Kirchner, and Schumann. March 1,
    1989.
Jerome Rose, piano and the New World String Quartet.
    Henri Dutilleux, John Alden Carpenter, and Brahms.
    April 21, 1989.

The Mendelssohn String Quartet. Mozart, Schnittke, and
    Mendelssohn. October 16, 1989.
The Nicholas and Robert Mann Duo. Spohr, Prokofiev,
    Shapey, and Bartók. December 8, 1989.

PUBLICATIONS

Hugh Amory, *First Impressions: Printing in Cambridge,
    1639–1989.* Cambridge: Harvard University, 1989. Exhi-
    bition catalogue.
Hugh Amory, *Stephen Day's First Type.* Cambridge: The
    Houghton Library, 1989. Exhibition keepsake.
M. D. Feld, *The First Roman Printers and the Idioms of
    Humanism.* Special issue of the *Harvard Library Bulle-
    tin.* Exhibition catalogue.
James Hankins, *Italian Humanists in Ten Manuscripts from
    the Houghton Library.* [Cambridge: Harvard College
    Library], 1989. Exhibition catalogue.
John A. Moore, *Nature in the New World.* Special issue of
    the *Harvard Library Bulletin.* Exhibition catalogue.
Catherine J. Johnson, *The Stage Art of Theodore Komisar-
    jevsky: An Exhibition in the Harvard Theatre Collection.*
    Introduction by Ernestine Stodelle Komisarjevsky
    Chamberlain. Special issue of the *Harvard Library Bul-
    letin,* n.s. 1 (1989).
Eugenia Parry Janis, *The Invention of Photography and Its
    Impact on Learning: The Collections of Harrison D. Hor-
    blit.* [Cambridge: Harvard College Library], November
    1989.

1990

In January, Eleanor M. Garvey retires as Philip
Hofer Curator of Printing and Graphic Arts.
She is succeeded by Anne Anninger, who re-
turns to Houghton after serving for seven years
as Curator of Special Collections and Associate
College Librarian at Wellesley College.

The Eleanor M. Garvey Visiting Fellowship
in Printing and Graphic Arts is established to
enable a distinguished scholar to work in the
department's collections for one month each
year. Cambridge designer Jean Evans is commissioned to create a new digital typeface in
Eleanor Garvey's honor. Other short-term visiting fellowships are established during the year:
the Stanley J. Kahrl Fellowship in Literary
Manuscripts, the Stanley J. Kahrl Fellowship in
Theatre History, the Howard D. Rothschild
Fellowship in Dance, the John M. Ward Fellowship in Dance and Music for the Theatre,
and two Fellowships funded by the American
Society for Eighteenth-Century Studies.

At a symposium moderated by Roderick Stinehour in conjunction with the exhibition "The Work of Stephen Harvard," John Benson, Jerry Kelly and Julian Waters discuss the problems and challenges of computer type design. Harvard, who died in 1988, designed several of the publications of the Department of Printing and Graphic Arts and was the author of *An Italic Copybook* (1981), based on a manuscript by Bernardino Cataneo in the Department of Printing and Graphic Arts.

Richard Wendorf conducts a six-week seminar for college teachers on Bibliography and Portraiture, sponsored by the National Endowment for the Humanities.

Reinhold Brinkmann teaches Music 218v, Twentieth-Century Music, based on the recently acquired papers of Rudolf Kolisch.

The Library is closed for a week in September and again in November during major renovations to the heating and air-handling systems.

Glory, a major motion picture, is based on the Robert Gould Shaw papers. An exhibition of selected items in the Ground Floor proves tremendously popular and is continued into 1991.

Volume VIII of the *BAL* (Charles Warren Stoddard to Susan Bogart Warner) is published in March.

Acquisitions include an eighteenth-century Italian optical box, used for viewing topographical prints, and contemporary artists' books by Timothy Ely and Ken Campbell. A large group of Norwegian decorated papers by H. M. Refsum (1859–1936) is added to the Rosamond B. Loring Collection. On December 4, Alain Elkann, Italian novelist and biographer, presents the cassette tape of his interview with Alberto Moravia to the Harvard Library. The tape is received by Richard Wendorf on behalf of the Houghton Library.

Harvard University Press publishes a facsimile of John Keats's poetry in Houghton, edited by Jack Stillinger, with an introduction by Helen Vendler.

Arthur Amory Houghton, Jr. dies.

Cornelius G. Buttimer publishes a catalogue of Houghton's Irish manuscripts.

Eleanor M. Garvey. *Photo by Diane Asséo Griliches.*

Helmut N. Friedlaender establishes the Helmut N. Friedlaender Book Fund. The Harrison D. Horblit Fund for the History of Science is established by Mrs. Harrison Horblit in memory of her husband. Melvin R. Seiden, '52 establishes the Joan Nordell Fund in the Harvard Theatre Collection.

EXHIBITIONS

Exhibition Room

European City Views by Thomas Shotter Boys, 1803–1874
The Work of Stephen Harvard, 1948–1988
Thomas Hollis and the Harvard College Library
Ivory Diptych Sundials, 1580–1750: Instruments and Books from the Wheatland Collection

Amy Lowell Room

Heine Books and Manuscripts
Visions of Antarctica
Holmes at Harvard: An Exhibition of Works from the Speckled Band's Collection and other Collections at the Houghton Library
John Ashbery, a Small Selection from the Voluminous Papers of the 1989–1990 C. E. Norton Lecturer

Selections of Books and Manuscripts for Houghton's
  Fourth Librarian
Selections from the William Empson Papers
W. E. B. DuBois: Correspondence in the Collections of the
  Houghton Library
Hemingway at Houghton: An Exhibition of Hemingway
  Papers and Publications for the Hemingway Society
T. B. Meteyard Designs
Literary Fragments, an Exhibition for the Jane Austen
  Society

Keats Room

Keats Manuscripts, an Exhibition in Honor of Helen
  Vendler, Jack Stillinger and the Harvard University Press

Ground Floor

Frank O'Hara, a Selection of Manuscripts Lent by Mau-
  reen O'Hara
"Tell it with Pride to the World": Robert Gould Shaw and
  the Massachusetts 54th

Theatre Collection

Robert Redington Sharpe
Under the Christmas Tree: Children's Plays

Widener Memorial Room

Seeing the World Through Children's Eyes: Children's
  Books Illustrated by Kate Greenaway from the Harry
  Elkins Widener Collection
Artist Books of the Kaldewey Press

LECTURES

Eleanor M. Garvey, "'My Hobby, Books, Has Turned Into
  a Profession:' Philip Hofer and the Graphic Arts." Jan-
  uary 10, 1990.
I Bernard Cohen, "From the Heart of Darkness to White-
  ness: Visions of Antarctica in Imagination and Reality."
  Fortieth George Parker Winship Lecture. April 16, 1990.
Rosamond McKitterick, "Carolingian Book Production:
  Some Problems." May 1, 1990.
John Haffenden, "William Empson." Co-sponsored by the
  Harvard Department of English.
Roderick Stinehour, John Benson, Jerry Kelly, Julian
  Waters, "Lettering Today." Symposium in conjunction
  with the exhibition "The Work of Stephen Harvard."
  May 9, 1990.
Joseph Krüse, "Heine and the French Revolution." Co-
  sponsored by the Harvard Department of Germanic
  Languages and Literature. May 16, 1990.
David Landes, "The Time of Our Lives: The Importance
  of Time Measurement in Western Civilization." Octo-
  ber 9, 1990.
John Halperin, "Jane Austen's Anti-Romantic Fragment:
  Some Notes on *Sanditon*." Co-sponsored by the Jane
  Austen Society. October 25, 1990.
Gunnar Kaldewey, "Artist Books of the Kaldewey Press."
  Philip and Frances Hofer Lecture. November 28, 1990.

CONCERTS

Ilton Wjuniski, harpsichord and Emanuele Segre, guitar.
  Couperin, Weiss, Villa-Lobos, Paganini, and Boccheri-
  ni. March 23, 1990.
Veronica Jochum, piano and the New World String Quar-
  tet. Hugo Wolf, Brahms, and Schumann. April 18, 1990.
Michael Zaretsky, viola and Randall Hodgkinson, piano.
  Schubert, Hindemith, Glinka, and Shostakovich. No-
  vember 12, 1990.

PUBLICATIONS

Emma Hamilton's Attitudes. Facsimile of Frederick Reh-
  berg's publication of 1794. Introduction by Richard
  Wendorf. Keepsake in honor of Eleanor M. Garvey.
  Cambridge: The Houghton Library, 1990.
David P. Becker, *The Work of Stephen Harvard, 1948–1988:
  A Life in Letters.* Cambridge: Department of Printing and
  Graphic Arts, The Houghton Library, Harvard College
  Library, 1990.
Evro Layton, *Five Centuries of Books and Manuscripts in
  Modern Greek.* Cambridge: Harvard College Library,
  1990.
Roger E. Stoddard, "Real Books Imagined, Imaginary
  Catalogue Realized: For a Bookseller and His Friends,"
  in *Voor Anton Gerits.* Amsterdam, 1990. Includes check-
  list of the 1980 Publishing History exhibition.
Arnold Wengrow, *Robert Redington Sharpe: The Life of a
  Theatre Designer.* Cambridge: Harvard Theatre Collec-
  tion: Harvard College Library, 1990.
Roger E. Stoddard, "Latin Verse of the Renaissance: the
  Collection and Exhibition at the Houghton Library,"
  Harvard Library Bulletin, n.s. 1: 2 (1990), 19–38. Cata-
  logue of the 1986 exhibition.

1991

Building renovations continue with the installation of new energy-efficient, ultraviolet screen
windows. During the installation of these windows in the Reading Room, reader services are
again (see 1987) transferred to the Exhibition
Room and continue without interruption.
Many public areas of the Library are repainted
in a new harmonious color scheme for the first
time in fifty years.

The Houghton Mifflin Company present
their papers and the Ralph Waldo Emerson
Memorial Association present his journals in
honor of Houghton's fiftieth anniversary; these
papers have been on deposit for nearly fifty
years. An additional visiting fellowship (see
1990), the Houghton Mifflin Fellowship in
Publishing History, is established. The seven
fellowships established in 1990 are awarded for
the first time.

The Harvard Theatre Collection receives the bequest of Howard D. Rothschild, a major collection devoted to Diaghilev's Ballets Russes and a substantial endowment. In July, the Theatre Collection takes ownership of the Edwin Binney 3rd bequest, the largest private collection of prints and drawings on dance.

Dr. Myron Hofer gives *Le corbeau,* Stéphane Mallarmé's translation of "The Raven," with illustrations by Édouard Manet, to the Department of Printing and Graphic Arts.

The Johnsonians hold their annual dinner at the Houghton Library on September 13.

Work is begun on an on-line catalogue of all the drawings in Printing and Graphic Arts and the Manuscript Department.

Volume IX of the *BAL* (Edward Noyes Westcott to Elinor Wylie) is published.

Volume III of the *STC,* containing indexes of printers and of places other than London with cumulative addenda and corrigenda for the two previous volumes, is published in May. For the third and final volume of the *STC,* Katharine F. Pantzer uses a computer to produce camera-ready copy for the printer. She is awarded a Guggenheim Fellowship for her proposal, "Probing some of the mysteries of printing in English 1523–1558."

The first volume of James E. Walsh's catalogue of Harvard incunabula, for the German speech-area (including Strasbourg) appears.

The Work of Stephen Harvard, 1948–1988, by David P. Becker, receives first place in Division I of the Katharine Kyes Leab and Daniel L. Leab "American Book Prices Current" Exhibition Catalogue Awards for 1991.

Melvin R. Seiden is appointed Honorary Curator of the Visual Arts in the College Library. Charles A. Rheault, Jr. is appointed Honorary Curator of Modern Typography in the College Library. John M. Ward is appointed Honorary Curator of Dance and Music for the Theatre in the College Library.

EXHIBITIONS

Exhibition Room

Edizioni dell'Elefante
Thomas Hollis and the Harvard College Library
Bibliotheca Bibliographica Breslaueriana: A Selection of

Classic Works of Bibliography in Fine Bindings from the Fifteenth Century to the Present Day from the Collection of B. H. Breslauer
Decorated Book Papers, 1890–1940
Robert Graff, Book Collector
Herman Melville, 1819–1891
The Building of the House Reflected in its Records: A Sampling of the Papers of the Houghton Mifflin Company and its Affiliates

Amy Lowell Room

Eighteenth-Century Optical Views and Viewers
Lauro de Bosis, on the Sixtieth Anniversary of his Flight
Hommage à Marguerite Yourcenar

Theatre Collection

Serge Diaghilev and the Ballets Russes
Students on Stage: A Year in the Theatre
Photographs from the Frederick R. Koch, '55 Collection

Widener Memorial Room

Goya and the Satirical Print in England and on the Continent
The Bow & Arrow Press: A Show of Recent Work
Vizetelly Drawings
Close of the Century
Letterpress Guild of New England: Recent Work
Philip Hofer Prize in Book Collecting

Theodore Roosevelt Gallery

TR in Cartoon: *The Verdict,* 1898–1900

Lammot Du Pont Copeland Gallery

A Selection of German Manuscripts from the Houghton Library for the Opening of Werner Otto Hall

LECTURES

Bernard H. Breslauer, "Master Jean Mallart, Royal Poet & Calligrapher & Sovereign Water Diviner." Forty-first George Parker Winship Lecture. February 21, 1991.

Lotte Hellinga, "Printing Press Practice in Fifteenth-Century Europe." Forty-second George Parker Winship Lecture. March 14, 1991.

David McKitterick, "The Word, the Law and the Profits: the Bible in Seventeenth-Century England." Forty-third George Parker Winship Lecture. March 28, 1991.

Natalie Zemon Davis, "Scholars and Censorship: Learned Periodicals during the German Occupation of France, 1940–1944." Forty-fourth George Parker Winship Lecture. April 16, 1991.

Claire Van Vliet, "Papers and Books at the Janus Press." Philip and Frances Hofer Lecture. May 15, 1991.

Paula R. Backscheider, "Gothic Drama, the Visual Arts, and Portrayals of Actresses." May 2, 1991.

Christian Jouhard, "Power and Literature in the Seventeenth Century: The Case of the *Querelle du Cid.*" Jointly sponsored by the Department of Romance Literatures, The Department of History, The Committee on Degrees in History and Literature, and the Houghton Library. October 21, 1991.

Ann Hechle, "Insight and Outlook." Jointly sponsored by the Lettering Arts Guild and the Department of Printing and Graphic Arts. October 24,1991.

Elizabeth Eisenstein, "Grub Street Abroad." Forty-sixth George Parker Winship Lecture. October 30, 1991.

Terry Belanger, "Education for Books as Physical Objects." Forty-seventh George Parker Winship Lecture. November 12, 1991.

Mark Olson, Barbara Cash, Scott Vile, Ilse Buchert Nesbitt, and John Kristensen (moderator), "Letterpress Publishing Roundtable." Sponsored by the Letterpress Guild of New England and the Department of Printing and Graphic Arts. November 15, 1991.

Nicholas Pickwood, "The Uses of Bookbinding History." Forty-eighth George Parker Winship Lecture. December 4, 1991.

CONCERTS

The Chilingirian String Quartet. Mozart, Bartók, Schubert, and Beethoven. January 7, 1991.

David Golub, piano; Mark Kaplan, violin; Colin Carr, cello. Mozart, Smetana, and Beethoven. February 8, 1991.

Robert Taub, piano. Beethoven and Brahms, April 10, 1991.

Daniel Stepner, violin, and John Gibbons, fortepiano. Mozart. October 17, 1991.

Lucy Stoltzman, violin, Toby Hoffman, viola, Ronald Thomas, cello, and Robert Taub, piano. Debussy, Beethoven, and Brahms. November 1, 1991.

PUBLICATIONS

Edizioni dell'Elefante, 1964–1990: Work of the Roman Publishers Enzo and Benedetta Crea. Cambridge: Harvard College Library, 1991. Exhibition catalogue

Roger E. Stoddard, *Bibliotheca Bibliographica Breslaueriana: A Selection of Classic Works of Bibliography in Fine Bindings from the Fifteenth Century to the Present Day from the Collection of B. H. Breslauer on Exhibition.* Cambridge: Harvard College Library, 1991. Exhibition catalogue.

Billy in the Darbies: A Facsimile from the Manuscript of Herman Melville's Billy Budd, Sailor. Ed. Dennis Marnon. [Cambridge]: The Houghton Library, 1991. Exhibition keepsake.

Hommage à Marguerite Yourcenar. Cambridge: The Houghton Library, 1991. Exhibition checklist.

A Plate Inventory of 1878, Valuing the Assets of James R. Osgood & Co. at the Time of That Firm's Merger with Hurd and Houghton to Form Houghton, Osgood & Co. [Cambridge: Houghton Library], 1991. Exhibition keepsake.

Carolyn Jakeman.

STAFF LISTS

Assembling the names of fifty years of Houghton personnel proved to be a far larger task than anticipated. Records were far from complete and not very accessible. Job titles that appear in directories are often inaccurate and dates are approximate. "Casual" employees, students and volunteers are usually omitted. It has therefore not been possible, as we once hoped, to include everyone who ever worked for the Houghton Library.

If the following lists are imperfect, however, they do reflect in a general way the changes that have taken place in the different departments. The lists are organized in ten-year segments in order to suggest who worked with whom. Changes of department are indicated only in the decade in which they occurred. Comprehensive employment histories within a department are given for those employees whose service spanned more than one decade. Dates are as accurate as our sources permitted.

1942–1951

OFFICE OF THE LIBRARIAN

William A. Jackson, *Assistant Librarian,* 1942–
John E. Alden, *Assistant,* 1942–1947
G.W. Cottrell, Jr., *Assistant,* 1942–1946
William H. Bond, *Assistant,* 1946–1948 *(to MS Dept.)*
Leslie M. Oliver, *Assistant,* 1948–
Frederica H. Oldach, *Secretary,* 1942– ; *Research Assistant,* 1949–
Marguerite A. Cronin, *Secretary,* 1949–1950
Mary Leone Haight, *Secretary,* 1950–

CATALOGUE DEPARTMENT

William H. McCarthy, Jr., *in charge,* 1942–1948
Mildred E. Nickerson, 1942– ; *in charge,* 1948– ; *Subject Specialist,* 1951–
James E. Walsh, 1947– ; *Associate,* 1948– ; *Head,* 1951–
Robert F. Metzdorf, *Associate,* 1949–1951
Phyllis B. Chase, *Cataloguer,* 1942–1947
Vinton A. Dearing, *Cataloguer,* 1947–1949
Mary Winslow, *Manuscript Cataloguer,* 1942–1949
M. Alice Cauchon, *Typist,* 1942–
Mary Garoian, 1942–?
John D. Constable, 1942–1946
Pearl Hekimian, 1942–1946
Dorothy F. Forsythe, 1947–1948
Mary Shea Goulart, 1947–1948 *(to Reading Room)*

MANUSCRIPT DEPARTMENT (EST. 1948)

William H. Bond, *Curator,* 1948– *(from Lib'ns Office)*
Jean G. Briggs, *Assistant,* 1948–1949 *(to Reading Room)*
Winifred Cadbury, *Assistant,* 1949–1951
Helen B. Ritchie, *Assistant,* 1951–
Lillian A. Adamian, 1949–1951
Klara E. Mora, 1951–

READING ROOM

Carolyn E. Jakeman, *in charge,* 1942–
William H. Power, 1942–1946
Eleanor Townsend, 1942–1946
Evelyn M. Williams, 1942–1946
Elinor Nolan, 1946–1948
Doris C. Powell, 1946–1948
Mary Shea Goulart, 1948– *(from Cat. Dept.)*
Joan F. Williams, 1948–1949
Jean G. Briggs, 1949–1950 *(from MS Dept.)*
Paul A. Sebastian, 1949–1950
Harold M. Terrell, 1949–1951
Barbara K. Hobbs, 1950–1951
Helen H. Pierce, 1951–
Thomas Matthews, *Doorman,* 1942–

DEPARTMENT OF PRINTING AND GRAPHIC ARTS

Philip Hofer, *Curator,* 1942–
William E. Baldwin, *Director of Publications,* 1942–?
Frederica H. Oldach, *Secretary,* 1942–1946
Louise K. Reynolds, *Secretary,* 1946–1948
Nancy F. Smith, *Secretary,* 1948–1949
Martha T. Sugi, *Secretary,* 1949–1950
Laura A. Master, *Secretary,* 1950–
Adriana R. Salem, 1942–1948
Arnold Weinberger, 1942–1950

THEATRE COLLECTION (MOVES TO HOUGHTON IN 1947)

William B. Van Lennep, *Curator,* 1947–
Miss Johnston, 1947
Cynthia Baker, 1947–1948
Mary Reardon Keating, *Assistant,* 1948–

KEATS ROOM

Mabel A. E. Steele, *Curator,* 1942–

1952–1961

OFFICE OF THE LIBRARIAN

William A. Jackson, *Assistant Librarian,* 1942–; *Librarian,* 1957–

Leslie M. Oliver, *Assistant,* 1948–1954

William B. Todd, *Assistant,* 1954–1958

Roger E. Stoddard, *Assistant,* 1958–1961

Kenneth Carpenter, *Assistant,* 1961–1962 *(from Reading Room)*

Frederica H. Oldach, *Secretary,* 1942– ; *Research Assistant,* 1949–1953

Anne W. Henry, *Research Assistant,* 1953–1960

Rosemary Boris, *Research Assistant,* 1957–1959

Myra Brenner, *Research Assistant,* 1959

Ann Cox-Johnson, *Research Assistant,* 1959–1960

Janet Eagleson Critics, *Research Assistant,* 1960–

Sarah Grant, *Research Assistant,* 1961–

Miriam T. Erickson, *Secretary,* 1952–1953

Mary E. Antich, *Secretary,* 1953–1954

Elinor Halsted, *Secretary,* 1954–1957

Jean C. Stump, *Secretary,* 1957–1958

Margery B. Dakin, *Secretary,* 1958–1960

Margaret Brooks, *Secretary,* 1960–1961

Jeri Mignault, *Secretary,* 1961

Marthena Scollon, *Typist,* 1961

CATALOGUE DEPARTMENT

James E. Walsh, 1947– ; *Associate,* 1948– ; *Head,* 1951–

Mildred E. Nickerson, 1942– ; *in charge,* 1948– ; *Subject Specialist,* 1951–

William M. Howie, *Cataloguer,* 1952–1954

Daniel E. Whitten, *Cataloguer,* 1956–

Ruth Mortimer, *Cataloguer for Printing and Graphic Arts,* 1957–

M. Alice Cauchon, *Typist,* 1942–

Carol M. Fields, *Typist,* 1952–1954

Harold M. Terrell, *Typist,* 1954– *(from Reading Room)*

MANUSCRIPT DEPARTMENT

William H. Bond, *Curator,* 1948–

Helen B. Ritchie, *Assistant,* 1951–1953

Marilyn S. Schultz, *Assistant,* 1953–1954

Iris I. Teragawa, *Assistant,* 1954–1956

Margaret L. Holmstead, 1952–1956

Clara L. Stiles, 1956–1957

Cornelia Brayton, 1957–1958

Harriet Yarbrough, 1958–1959

Susan Stanwood Clark, 1959–1961

Georgette Bandurian, 1961

READING ROOM

Carolyn E. Jakeman, *in charge,* 1942–

Mary Shea Goulart, 1948–1954

Mary K. Daehler, 1952–1957

Harold M. Terrell, 1949–1954 *(to Cat. Dept.)*

Ann W. Craig, 1954–1955

Julie Johnson Sirois, 1956–1960

Alix M. Hawkins, 1957–1959

Kenneth Carpenter, 1959–1961 *(to Lib'ns Office)*

Jean Artin, 1960–1961

Joseph P. McCarthy, 1961–

Katherine Livingston, 1961

Cynthia Naylor, 1960–

Thomas Matthews, *Doorman,* 1942–

DEPARTMENT OF PRINTING AND GRAPHIC ARTS

Philip Hofer, *Curator,* 1942–

Eleanor M. Garvey, *Assistant,* 1953–

Laura A. Master, *Secretary,* 1950–1953

THEATRE COLLECTION

William B. Van Lennep, *Curator,* 1947–1960 *(retired)*

Helen D. Willard, *Curator,* 1960–

Mary Reardon Keating, *Assistant,* 1948–1959

Audrey Hosford, 1959–

KEATS ROOM

Mabel A. E. Steele, *Curator,* 1942–

1962–1971

OFFICE OF THE LIBRARIAN

William A. Jackson, *Assistant Librarian,* 1942–; *Librarian,* 1957–1964†
William H. Bond, *Acting Librarian,* 1964 *(from MS Dept.); Librarian,* 1965–
Roger E. Stoddard, *Assistant,* 1958–1961; *Assistant Librarian,* 1965– ; *Associate Librarian,* 1969–
Martin Faigel, *Assistant,* 1962–1964
Sidney E. Ives, *Assistant,* 1964– ; *Assistant to the Librarian,* 1965– ; *Acquisitions Bibliographer,* 1966–
Janet Eagleson Critics, *Research Assistant,* 1960–
Sarah Grant, *Research Assistant,* 1961–1962
Katharine F. Pantzer, *Research Assistant,* 1962– ; *Research Bibliographer,* 1964–
Suellen Mutchow, *Research Assistant,* 1966–1970
Karen Nelson, *Secretary,* 1962–1964
Luise B. Mallinger, *Secretary,* 1964–1967
Katherine Paranya, *Secretary,* 1967–1969
Marcia L. Due, *Secretary,* 1969–1970
Karen B. Boeyink, *Secretary,* 1970–62
Gertraude Roth, *Typist,* 1962–1964
Mary Ann Katsiane, *Typist,* 1964–1966
Kausalya Shenbagam, *Typist,* 1966–1967
Duresamin Jan, *Typist,* 1967–1969
Susan H. R. Schcolnik, *Typist,* 1969–1970
John Weeks, *Typist,* 1970

CATALOGUE DEPARTMENT

James E. Walsh, 1947– ; *Associate,* 1948– ; *Head,* 1951– ; *Keeper of Printed Books,* 1971–
Mildred E. Nickerson, 1942– ; *in charge,* 1948– ; *Subject Specialist,* 1951–1970 *(retired)*
Daniel E. Whitten, *Cataloguer,* 1956–
Ruth Mortimer, *Cataloguer for Printing and Graphic Arts,* 1957–
Rita Hausammann, *Cataloguer,* 1964–1968
Jeffrey E. Marshall, *Cataloguer,* 1969–
John Lancaster, *Cataloguer,* 1970–
M. Alice Cauchon, *Typist,* 1942–1971 *(retired)*
Harold M. Terrell, *Typist,* 1954–
Cynthia Naylor, 1962– *(from Reading Room)*

MANUSCRIPT DEPARTMENT

William H. Bond, *Curator,* 1948–1964 *(to Lib'ns Office)*
Richard H. Rouse, *Cataloguer,* 1962–1963
Rodney G. Dennis, III, *Cataloguer,* 1963– ; *Curator,* 1965–
Donna Ferguson Packer, *Cataloguer,* 1965–1968
Suzanne Howard Currier, *Cataloguer,* 1970–
Judith Scoville, 1962–1964
Barbara DiAdamo, 1964–1965
Joan Fleming, *Secretary*
Therese Moore, *Secretary,* 1965–1966
Robyn Parris, *Secretary,* 1966–1967
Josephine Tournabane, *Secretary,* 1967–1968
Mary W. Coleman, *Secretary,* 1968–1969
Carmen Joseph, 1970–1971; *Secretary,* 1971
Rosemary Dwyer, 1969–1970
Gail Fulkerson, 1970–1971
Margaret Keller, *Typist,* 1971

READING ROOM

Carolyn E. Jakeman, *in charge,* 1942–; *Supervisor,* 1964–; *Assistant Librarian for Reference,* 1965–
Cynthia Naylor, 1960–1962 *(to Cat. Dept.)*
Joseph P. McCarthy, 1961–
Barbara Bolster, 1962–1964
Michael Flynn, 1964–1966
Carol D. Goodman, 1964–1966
Mary Frances Hickey, 1964–1965
Joseph Sullivan, 1964–1967
Christie Ricker, 1965–1967
Judith Andra, 1966–1967
J. Norton Cabell, 1966–1967
Frank Cox, 1967–1971
John J. Connell, 1967–
Marte Shaw, 1967–1969; 1971–
Anita Stanley, 1967–1968
Jannell Smith Jensen, 1968–1970
Suzanne Flandreau, 1969–1971
Linda Conolly, 1970–1971
Hinda F. Sklar, 1971– *(from Theatre Coll.)*
Jill Kahran, 1971
Toni Boldrick, 1971
Thomas Matthews, *Doorman,* 1942–1963 *(retired)*

DEPARTMENT OF PRINTING
AND GRAPHIC ARTS

Philip Hofer, *Curator,* 1942–1968
Peter A. Wick, *Associate Curator,* 1967– ; *Curator,* 1968–
Eleanor M. Garvey, *Assistant,* 1953– ; *Assistant Curator,*
    1961– ; *Associate Curator,* 1968–
Joyce Senders, *Secretary,* 1964–1965
Catherine Pawlcyn, *Secretary,* 1965–1966
Susan Kashiwa, *Secretary,* 1966–1968
Karen H. Rogers, *Secretary,* 1968–1969
Priscilla Barker, *Secretary,* 1970–?
Adele Wilson

THEATRE COLLECTION

Helen D. Willard, *Curator,* 1960–
Arnold Wengrow, *Assistant Curator,* 1966–1968
Jeanne T. Newlin, *Assistant Curator,* 1968– ; *Associate
    Curator,* 1971–
Audrey Hosford, 1959–1964
Penelope D. Hull, 1964–1966
Annaliese Munetic, 1964–1965
Mildred Williams, 1965–1966
Susan L. Orkin, *Secretary,* 1967–1968
Jean Finley, *Secretary,* 1968–1969
Mary Jo Poburko, *Secretary,* 1969–1970
Hinda F. Sklar, *Secretary,* 1970–1971 *(to Reading Room)*
Pamela Rowe, 1968–1970
Gary Abbott, 1970–1971
Martha R. Mahard, 1971–

KEATS ROOM (CLOSED, 1969–1971)

Mabel A. E. Steele, *Curator,* 1942–1964
Lynn Fairfield, 1965–1968
Rae Ann Nager, *Curator,* 1971–

HARRY ELKINS WIDENER MEMORIAL ROOMS

William H. Bond, *Curator,* 1969–1970
Marte Shaw, *Curator,* 1970–
Jill Karhan, *Assistant Curator,* 1970–1971
Harold L. Coffey, *Guard,* 1970–

THEODORE ROOSEVELT COLLECTION

Gregory C. Wilson, *Curator,* 1968–1971
Wallace F. Dailey, *Curator,* 1971–

1972–1981

OFFICE OF THE LIBRARIAN

William H. Bond, *Acting Librarian, 1964– ; Librarian, 1965–*

Roger E. Stoddard, *Assistant, 1958–1961; Assistant Librarian, 1965– ; Associate Librarian, 1969–*

Sidney E. Ives, *Assistant, 1964– ; Assistant to the Librarian, 1965– ; Acquisitions Bibliographer, 1966–1980*

Katharine F. Pantzer, *Assistant, 1962– ; Research Bibliographer, 1964–*

Janet Eagleson Critics, *Research Assistant, 1960–1975*

Blanche T. Ebeling-Koning, *Acquisitions Bibliographer, 1980–*

Virginia L. Smyers-Zern, *Acquisitions Assistant, 1972–1975*

Anne M. Anninger, *Acquisitions Assistant, 1975–1976 (to Cat. Dept.)*

Danial C. Elliott, *Acquisitions Assistant, 1976–1978*

Reed A. Boland, *Acquisitions Assistant, 1978–1980*

Mary F. Daniel, *Acquisitions Assistant, 1980–1981*

Alan D. Krieger, *Acquisitions Assistant, 1981*

Karen B. Boeyink, *Secretary, 1970–1978*

Helen A. Sahagian, *Secretary, 1978–1979*

Paula Balik, *Secretary, 1979–1980*

Elsa A. Passera, *Secretary, 1980–*

CATALOGUE DEPARTMENT

James E. Walsh, *1947– ; Associate, 1948– ; Head, 1951– ; Keeper of Printed Books, 1971–*

Ruth Mortimer, *Cataloguer for Printing and Graphic Arts, 1957–1975*

Daniel E. Whitten, *Cataloguer, 1956–1972†*

Jeffrey E. Marshall, *Cataloguer, 1969–1972 (to Theatre Coll.)*

John Lancaster, *Cataloguer, 1970–1976*

Lawrence Lipson, *Cataloguer, 1972–1973*

Hugh Amory, *Cataloguer, 1973–*

Mollie Della Terza, *Cataloguer, 1973–*

Lavinia De Nood, *Cataloguer, 1975–1976*

Anne M. Anninger, *Cataloguer, 1976– (from Lib'ns Office)*

Laszlo Dienes, *Cataloguer, 1976–1978*

Scott D. Ward, *Cataloguer, 1978–*

Harold M. Terrell, *Typist, 1954–*

Cynthia Naylor, *1962–*

Lorraine Murphy, *1972–1973*

Mary Cargill, *1974–1975*

MANUSCRIPT DEPARTMENT

Rodney G. Dennis, III, *Cataloguer, 1963– ; Curator, 1965–*

Suzanne Howard Currier, *Cataloguer, 1970–1981*

Patrick Miehe, *1972– ; Curatorial Associate, 1974– ; Cataloguer, 1976–1981*

Elizabeth A. Falsey, *Cataloguer, 1979–*

George Nakašidze, *Consultant on the Georgian Archive, 1974–1979*

Rosaria Forlani, *Secretary, 1972–1973*

Egle Zygas, *Secretary, 1974–1975*

Betty Blake, *Secretary, 1975–1978*

Virginia A. James, *Secretary, 1978–1979*

Bridget Carr Blagbrough, *Secretary, 1981–*

Barbara A. Filipac, *1979–1980*

Jane Richards, *1972–1973*

Caryl Johnston, *1974–1975*

Sharon L. Miller, *1975–1978*

Catherine M. Compton, *1978–1980 (to Reading Room)*

Leigh Clark, *1980–1981*

Jane R. Coleman, *1980–1981*

Vicki Denby, *1981–*

READING ROOM

Carolyn E. Jakeman, *in charge, 1942–; Supervisor, 1964–; Assistant Librarian for Reference, 1965–1976 (retired)*

Marte Shaw, *1967–1969; 1971– ; Curator, 1976–1979*

F. Thomas Noonan, *Curator, 1980–*

Deborah B. Kelley, *1972– ; Assistant Reference Librarian, 1975–1980*

John J. Connell, *1967–1973*

William Anthony, *1972–1973*

Joseph P. McCarthy, *1961– ; Supervisor of the Stack, 1972–1974*

Brian Bernhardt, *1975–?*

Dennis C. Marnon, *1975– ; Supervisor of the Stack, 1980–*

Jessica S. Owaroff, *1975–1980*

Bertrand R. Yourgrau, *1975–1978*

Martha Ramsey, *1976–1978*

Jean M. Seegraber, *1978–1980*

Catherine M. Compton, *1980– (from MS Dept.)*

Susan Halpert, *1980– ; Reference Librarian, 1981–*

Melanie M. Wisner, *1980–*

Hinda F. Sklar, *1971–1974*

Manuel M. Sadagursky, *Doorman, 1978–*

DEPARTMENT OF PRINTING AND GRAPHIC ARTS

Peter A. Wick, *Associate Curator,* 1967– ; *Curator,* 1968–1975

Eleanor M. Garvey, *Assistant,* 1953– ; *Assistant Curator,* 1961– ; *Associate Curator,* 1968– ; *Curator,* 1975–

David P. Becker, *Assistant Curator,* 1975–1980

Roger S. Wieck, *Assistant Curator,* 1980–

Nadya Dimitrov, *Secretary,* 1972–1973

Elizabeth R. Sahatjian, *Secretary,* 1974–1975

Susan London, *Secretary,* 1975–1978

Donna J. Surprenant, *Secretary,* 1978–1979

Susan Jackson, *Secretary,* 1979–

THEATRE COLLECTION

Helen D. Willard, *Curator,* 1960–1972 *(retired)*

Jeanne T. Newlin, *Assistant Curator,* 1968– ; *Associate Curator,* 1971– ; *Curator,* 1972–

Martha R. Mahard, 1971– ; *Curatorial Assistant,* 1976– ; *Assistant Curator,* 1980–

Jeffrey E. Marshall, *Cataloguer,* 1972–1979 *(from Cat. Dept.)*

Noreen C. Barnes, *Reading Room Supervisor,* 1980–1981

Andrea Perkins, *Secretary,* 1976–1978

Virginia E. Plant, *Secretary,* 1972–1974

Ellen K. Carlin, *Secretary,* 1974–1976

Anne Ames, 1978–1980

Lydia J. Orcutt, 1980–1981

KEATS ROOM

Rae Ann Nager, *Curator,* 1971–1980

HARRY ELKINS WIDENER MEMORIAL ROOMS

Marte Shaw, *Curator,* 1970–1979

F. Thomas Noonan, *Curator,* 1980–

Hinda F. Sklar, 1972–1973

Deborah B. Kelley, 1974–1976

Jessica S. Owaroff, 1975–1976

Harold L. Coffey, *guard,* 1970–1979

Max Lindahl, *guard,* 1980–

THEODORE ROOSEVELT COLLECTION

Wallace F. Dailey, *Curator,* 1971–

1982–1991

OFFICE OF THE LIBRARIAN

William H. Bond, *Acting Librarian, 1964– ; Librarian, 1965–1982 (retired)*

Lawrence Dowler, *Associate Librarian of Harvard College, 1982–1988; Librarian, 1985–1988*

Richard Wendorf, *Librarian, 1989–*

Roger E. Stoddard, *Assistant, 1958–1961; Assistant Librarian, 1965– ; Associate Librarian, 1969– ; Curator of Rare Books, 1986–*

Dennis C. Marnon, *Acquisitions Bibliographer, 1982– (from Reading Room); Administrative Officer, 1991–*

F. Thomas Noonan, *Research Services Librarian, 1984–1988 (from Reading Room)*

Katharine F. Pantzer, *Assistant, 1962– ; Research Bibliographer, 1964–1991 (retired)*

Blanche T. Ebeling-Koning, *Acquisitions Bibliographer, 1980–1982*

Bridget Carr Blagbrough, *Acquisitions Assistant, 1984–1986 (from MS Dept.)*

Peter Accardo, *Acquisitions Assistant, 1985–*

Lynn M. Shirey, *Acquisitions Assistant, 1986–1989*

Janet Scinto, *Acquisitions Assistant, 1989–*

Elsa Passera, *Secretary, 1980–1985*

Carol Fisher-Crosby, *Secretary, 1985–1989*

Roxana Breckner, *Staff Assistant, 1989–*

Andrea Stover, 1986–1991

CATALOGUE DEPARTMENT

James E. Walsh, 1947– ; *Associate, 1948– ; Head, 1958– ; Keeper of Printed Books, 1971–1988 (retired)*

Mollie Della Terza, *Cataloguer, 1973– ; Coordinator of Cataloguing, 1986– ; Head of Technical Services, 1988–*

Hugh Amory, *Cataloguer, 1973– ; Senior Cataloguer, 1990–*

Anne M. Anninger, *Cataloguer, 1976–1983*

Scott D. Ward, *Cataloguer, 1978–1985*

Patricia Jo Rogers, *Cataloguer, 1983*

Nancy Reinhardt, *Cataloguer, 1985–*

Mieczyslaw Buczkowski, *Cataloguer, 1988–1991*

Golda Steinberg, 1988–1991; *Cataloguer, 1991–*

Harold M. Terrell, *Typist, 1954–*

Cynthia Naylor, 1962–

Winthrop Pescosolido, 1989–

MANUSCRIPT DEPARTMENT

Rodney G. Dennis, III, *Cataloguer, 1963– ; Curator, 1965–1991 (retired)*

Elizabeth A. Falsey, *Cataloguer, 1979– ; Associate Curator, 1990–*

Laura Light, *Cataloguer, 1985–*

Barbara Wolff, *Cataloguer, 1989–*

Bonnie Salt, *Project Cataloguer, 1985–*

Caroline Preston, *Project Archivist, 1989–*

Bridget Carr Blagbrough, *Secretary, 1981–1984 (to Lib'ns Office)*

Madeleine Gosselin, *Staff Assistant, 1984–1985*

Emily Walhout, *Staff Assistant, 1986 (to Reading Room)*

Vicki Denby, *1981–1986; Curatorial Assistant, 1986–*

Caroline Bain, 1991–

MANUSCRIPT SURVEY AND GUIDE PROJECT

Lofton Wilson, *Project Librarian, 1984–1986*

Elisabeth Elkind, *Survey Archivist, 1985–1986*

Philip Eppard, *Survey Archivist, 1985–1986*

Elizabeth Pessek, *Survey Archivist, 1985–1986*

Forrestt Tellis, 1985–1986

Deborah White, 1985–1986

READING ROOM

F. Thomas Noonan, *Curator, 1980–1984 (to Lib'ns Office)*

James Lewis, *1984–1985; Curator, 1985–*

Susan Halpert, *1980– ; Reference Librarian, 1981–*

Dennis C. Marnon, *1975– ; Supervisor of the Stack, 1980–1982 (to Lib'ns Office)*

Melanie M. Wisner, 1980–

Catherine M. Compton, 1980–1985

Jennie Rathbun, 1984–

Dolores Velkley, 1984–1985

Joseph Callahan, 1985–1988

Sara Willis, 1985–1986

Judith Wilson, 1985–

Emily Walhout, *1986– (from MS Dept.)*

Denison Beach, 1988–

Laura Barton, 1988–

Manuel M. Sadagursky, *Doorman, 1978–1991 (retired)*

DEPARTMENT OF PRINTING
AND GRAPHIC ARTS

Eleanor M. Garvey, *Assistant,* 1953– ; *Assistant Curator,*
1968– ; *Associate Curator,* 1971– ; *Curator,* 1975–1984;
Philip Hofer Curator, 1984–1990 *(retired)*
Anne M. Anninger, *Philip Hofer Curator,* 1990–
Roger S. Wieck, *Assistant Curator,* 1980–1983
Nancy Finlay, *Assistant Curator,* 1983–1990; *Associate Cu-
rator,* 1990–1991
Laura Perine, *Staff Assistant,* 1984–1985
Lisa Moline, *Staff Assistant,* 1985–1987
Brenda Breed, *Staff Assistant,* 1987–
Sarah Scheffel, 1991–

THEATRE COLLECTION

Jeanne T. Newlin, *Assistant Curator,* 1968– ; *Associate
Curator,* 1971– ; *Curator,* 1972–
Martha R. Mahard, 1971– ; *Curatorial Assistant,* 1976– ;
Assistant Curator, 1980–1988
Catherine Johnson, *Assistant Curator,* 1988–1991
Marjorie Pepe, *Staff Assistant,* 1984–1988
Bistra Lankova, 1984–1986
Robert Wright, 1986–1989
Gavin McCormick, 1988–1989
Joseph G. Keller, *Reading Room Assistant,* 1989–
Brian Benoit, *Staff Assistant,* 1989–
Cari Rae Palmer, *Mellon Cataloger for the Dance,* 1990–

HARRY ELKINS WIDENER MEMORIAL ROOMS

F. Thomas Noonan, *Curator,* 1980–1988
James Lewis, *Curator,* 1988–

THEODORE ROOSEVELT COLLECTION

Wallace F. Dailey, *Curator,* 1971–

EXHIBITION CATALOGUES

Arno Werner, Master Bookbinder, comp. James E. Walsh. Cambridge: The Houghton Library, 1981.

The Art of Adding and The Art of Taking Away. Selections from John Updike's Manuscripts, comp. Elizabeth A. Falsey. Cambridge: Harvard College Library, 1987.

The Artist and the Book, 1860–1960 in Western Europe and the United States, comp. Eleanor M. Garvey; introd. by Philip Hofer. Cambridge: Department of Printing and Graphic Arts, Harvard College Library; and Boston: The Museum of Fine Arts, 1961; 2nd ed., 1972.

Artists of the Book in Boston, 1890–1910, comp. Nancy Finlay. Cambridge: Department of Printing and Graphic Arts, The Houghton Library, Harvard College Library, 1985.

The Bible in the Twelfth Century, comp. Laura Light. Cambridge: Harvard College Library, 1988.

Bibliotheca Bibliographica Breslaueriana: A Selection of Classic Works of Bibliography in Fine Bindings from the Fifteenth Century to the Present Day from the Collection of B. H. Breslauer on Exhibition, comp. Roger E. Stoddard. Cambridge: Harvard College Library, 1991.

Bibliotheca Chimærica: A Catalogue of an Exhibition of Catalogues of Imaginary Books, comp. William A. Jackson. Cambridge, 1962.

A Catalogue of an Exhibition of the Philip Hofer Bequest in the Department of Printing and Graphic Arts, comp. Eleanor Garvey, Nancy Finlay, Rodney G. Dennis, and others. Cambridge: Harvard College Library, 1988.

Collector's Choice: A Selection of Books and Manuscripts Given by Harrison D. Horblit to the Harvard College Library, comp. Owen Gingerich. Cambridge, 1983.

Conversations, or the Bas Bleu, comp. Sidney Ives. Cambridge: Harvard College Library, 1977.

Creating the Empire of Reason: Massachusetts Ratifies the United States Constitution. Cambridge: Harvard College Library, 1988. Catalogue of an exhibition of material from the Houghton Library.

Danish Literature: Saxo Grammaticus to Isak Dinesen, comp. Nancy S. Reinhardt. Cambridge: Harvard College Library, 1986.

The Dark Side of the Enlightenment, comp. F. Thomas Noonan. Cambridge: Harvard College Library, 1984.

Drawings for Book Illustration: The Hofer Collection, comp. David P. Becker. Cambridge: Department of Printing and Graphic Arts, The Houghton Library, 1980.

Dressing Broadway: Costume Designs of Lucinda Ballard. Cambridge: Harvard Theatre Collection, Harvard College Library, 1987.

Early Botanical Books: An Exhibit Celebrating the Centennial of the Arnold Arboretum 1872–1972. Cambridge, The Houghton Library [1972].

Edizioni dell'Elefante, 1964–1990: Work of the Roman Publishers Enzo and Benedetta Crea. Cambridge: Harvard College Library, 1991.

Erasmus on the 500th Anniversary of His Birth, comp. James E. Walsh. Cambridge: The Houghton Library, 1969.

Europe Informed: An Exhibition of Early Books which Acquainted Europe with the East, comp. Francis M. Rogers. Cambridge and New York, 1966.

An Exhibition of Books Designed by Charles Ricketts from the Collection of A. E. Gallatin. [Cambridge]: The Houghton Library, Harvard University, 1946.

An Exhibition of Books Published When They Were 21 or Younger by One Hundred Authors Who Later Became Famous, comp. William A. Jackson. Cambridge, 1961.

[An Exhibition of Music Manuscripts to Honor the Boston Symphony Orchestra]: Rodney G. Dennis, "An Exhibition of Music Manuscripts in the Houghton Library Prepared to Honor the BSO," *Harvard Library Bulletin,* 31 (1983), 88–95.

Fact and Fantasy: Illustrated Books from a Private Collection, comp. David P. Becker. Cambridge, Department of Printing and Graphic Arts, Harvard College Library, 1976.

[Fifty Novels in Manuscript]: Rodney G. Dennis, "An Exhibition of Manuscripts in the Houghton Library," *Manuscripts,* 18 (1966), 40–42.

First Impressions: Printing in Cambridge, 1639–1989, comp. Hugh Amory. Cambridge: Harvard University, 1989.

The First Roman Printers and the Idioms of Humanism, comp. M. D. Feld: special issue of the *Harvard Library Bulletin.*

Five Centuries of Books and Manuscripts in Modern Greek, comp. Evro Layton. Cambridge: Harvard College Library, 1990.

Four Hundred Years of Dance Notation. Cambridge: Harvard Theatre Collection, Harvard College Library, 1987.

[German Illustrated Books from the Sixteenth Century]: Roger S. Wieck, "An Exhibition of German Illustrated Books from the Sixteenth Century: The Gift of Philip Hofer," *Harvard Library Bulletin,* 29 (1981), 332–336.

Goethe, comp. James E. Walsh and Eugene M. Weber. Cambridge: Harvard College Library and the Goethe Institute of Boston, 1982.

H. H. Richardson and his Office, Selected Drawings. A Centennial of his Move to Boston 1874, comp. James F. O'Gorman; pref. by Peter A. Wick. [Cambridge]: Department of Printing and Graphic Arts, Harvard College Library, 1974.

He Has Long Outlived His Century. Catalogue of an exhibition of books and manuscripts collected by Mary and Donald Hyde, Arthur A. Houghton, Jr., Robert Metzdorf, Amy Lowell, Harold Murdock, Houghton Mifflin Co., and others. Cambridge: The Houghton Library, 1984.

The Houghton Library, 1942–1982: A Fortieth Anniversary Exhibition, comp. Roger E. Stoddard. Cambridge: The Houghton Library, 1982.

Illuminated and Calligraphic Manuscripts [comp. William H. Bond and Philip Hofer]. Cambridge: Harvard College, 1955.

The Invention of Photography and Its Impact on Learning: The Collections of Harrison D. Horblit, comp. Eugenia Parry Janis. [Cambridge: Harvard College Library], November 1989.

Italian Humanists in Ten Manuscripts from the Houghton Library, comp. James Hankins. [Cambridge]: The Houghton Library, 1989.

The Kilgour Collection of Russian Literature, comp. Roger E. Stoddard. Cambridge: The Houghton Library, 1977.

Late Medieval and Renaissance Illuminated Manuscripts 1350–1525 in the Houghton Library, comp. Roger S. Wieck. Cambridge: Department of Printing and Graphic Arts, Harvard College Library, 1983.

[Latin Verse of the Renaissance]: Roger E. Stoddard, "Latin Verse of the Renaissance: the Collection and Exhibition at the Houghton Library," *Harvard Library Bulletin,* n.s. 1: 2 (1990), 19–38.

Longing for the Ideal: Images of Marie Taglioni in the Romantic Ballet, comp. Edwin Binney, 3rd. Cambridge: Harvard Theatre Collection, Harvard College Library, 1984.

Luther 1483–1983, comp. James E. Walsh. Cambridge: Harvard College Library, 1983.

Manuscripts by Harvard Authors. Catalogue of an exhibition at the Houghton Library to celebrate the 350th Anniversary of the Founding of Harvard College Library, comp. Rodney G. Dennis. Cambridge, 1986.

Marks in Books, Illustrated and Explained, comp. Roger E. Stoddard. Cambridge: The Houghton Library, Harvard University, 1985.

[Materials for the Study of Publishing History]: Roger E. Stoddard, "Real books Imagined, Imaginary Catalogue Realized: For a Bookseller and his Friends," in *Voor Anton Gerits.* Amsterdam, 1990.

Nature in the New World, comp. John A. Moore. Special issue of the *Harvard Library Bulletin.*

New Books by Fielding, Commentary Toward an Exhibition, comp. Hugh Amory. Cambridge: The Houghton Library, 1987.

New Sweden and the Harvard College Library, 1636–1986, comp. Nancy S. Reinhardt. [Cambridge, 1988].

The Ostrih Bible 1580/81–1980/81: A Quadricentennial Exhibition. Cambridge: The Houghton Library, Harvard University, 1980.

The Player-King: Shakespeare's Histories on the Stage, pref. by Jeanne T. Newlin. Cambridge, 1974.

[Printing Types through Five Centuries]: Eleanor M. Garvey, "Printing Types through Five Centuries: An Exhibition Selected from the Bentinck-Smith Collections in the Department of Printing and Graphic Arts," *Harvard Library Bulletin,* 30 (1982), 349–354.

Pushkin and his Friends: The Making of a Literature and a Myth, comp. John E. Malmstad and William Mills Todd, III; ed. Hugh Amory. [Cambridge]: The Houghton Library, 1987.

Rara Astronomica, comp. Owen Gingerich. Cambridge, 1970.

Robert Redington Sharpe: The Life of a Theatre Designer, comp. Arnold Wengrow. Cambridge: Harvard Theatre Collection: Harvard College Library, 1990.

[A Selection of French Literary Manuscripts, 1600–1960]: Suzanne N. H. Currier, "An Exhibition of French Literary Manuscripts, 1600–1960," *Harvard Library Bulletin,* 29 (1981), 217–224.

Seventh International Congress of Bibliophiles Exhibition: Sidney E. Ives, *VII International Congress of Bibliophiles, Boston Program.* Cambridge, 1971. Includes the illustrated catalogue of the exhibition.

Shelley and his Circle: Additions to the Carl H. Pforzheimer Library 1957–1978. [Cambridge]: The Houghton Library, 1978.

Sixteenth-Century Architectural Books from Italy and France, comp. Peter A. Wick. Cambridge: Department of Printing and Graphic Arts, Harvard College Library, 1971.

Sources for Twentieth-Century Music History, comp. Helmut Hell, Sigrid von Moisy and Barbara Wolff. Munich and Cambridge, 1988. Catalogue of a joint exhibition of the Houghton Library and the Bayerische Staatsbibliothek.

Spanish and Portuguese Sixteenth-Century Books in the Department of Printing and Graphic Arts, comp. Anne Anninger. Cambridge: Harvard College Library, 1985.

The Stage Art of Theodore Komisarjevsky: An Exhibition in the Harvard Theatre Collection, comp. Catherine J. Johnson; introd. by Ernestine Stodelle Komisarjevsky Chamberlain: special issue of *Harvard Library Bulletin,* 37 (1989).

Tenniel's Alice: Drawings by Sir John Tenniel for Alice's Adventures in Wonderland and Through the Looking Glass, introd. by Eleanor M. Garvey and W. H. Bond. Cambridge: Department of Printing and Graphic Arts, Harvard College Library; and New York: The Metropolitan Museum of Art, 1978.

Theatre of Marvels: Popular Entertainments on Boulevard and Fairground. Cambridge: Harvard Theatre Collection, Harvard College Library, 1985.

The Turn of a Century, 1885–1910: Art Nouveau-Jugendstil Books, comp. Eleanor M. Garvey, Anne B. Smith, and Peter A. Wick. Cambridge: Department of Printing and Graphic Arts, The Houghton Library, Harvard University, 1970.

Twentieth Century Stage Design, comp. Helen D. Willard. Cambridge, 1972.

Ukrainian Incunabula, Manuscripts, Early Printed and Rare Books, comp. Edward Kasinec. Cambridge, 1970.

Vienna 1888–1938, comp. Eugene M. Weber and James E. Walsh. Cambridge: The Houghton Library, 1967.

William Dean Howells, 1837–1920: A Sesquicentennial Exhibition, comp. Michael Anesko. [Cambridge]: The Houghton Library, 1987.

The Work of Stephen Harvard, 1948–1988: A Life in Letters, comp. David P. Becker. Cambridge: Department of Printing and Graphic Arts, The Houghton Library, Harvard College Library, 1990.

INDEX

COLOPHON

THIS BOOK WAS SET IN ADOBE GARAMOND TYPES

AND WAS PRINTED ON MOHAWK SUPERFINE PAPER

AT THE OFFICE OF THE UNIVERSITY PUBLISHER

DESIGNED BY GINO LEE